# Paul Cuffe

# Paul Cuffe

## His Purpose, Partners and Properties

David C. Cole

Betty F. Slade

Richard Gifford

Illustrations by

Raymond C. Shaw

*Spinner Publications, Inc.*

New Bedford, Massachusetts

Spinner Publications, Inc., New Bedford, Massachusetts 02740
© 2020 Spinner Publications, Inc.
All Rights Reserved.

Text © David Cole
Original illustrations © Raymond C. Shaw
Printed in the United States of America.

This publication is made possible by the Westport Cultural Council through grants
from the Helen Ellis Charitable Trust administered by Bank of America.

Library of Congress Cataloging-in-Publication Data

Names: Cole, David C. (David Chamberlin), 1928- author. | Slade, Betty F., author. | Gifford,
  Richard, author. | Shaw, Raymond C., illustrator.
  Title: Paul Cuffe : his purpose, partners and properties / David Cole, Betty F. Slade,
  Richard Gifford ; illustrations by Raymond C. Shaw.
Description: Westport, Massachusetts : Spinner Publications, Inc., [2020] | Includes
  bibliographical references and index. | Summary: "Paul Cuffe evolved from an
  unschooled child living within the Wampanoag community on the South Coast of
  Massachusetts into a charismatic and inspirational leader widely known and respected
  on both sides of the Atlantic. He was born on the island of Cuttyhunk in 1759, the son of
  a freed slave and a Native American woman. He was largely self-educated but attained
  a high level of literacy and writing abilities. He learned other skills such as navigation
  and shipbuilding through on-the-job experience. Within the short lifespan of fifty-eight
  years, Paul Cuffe became a widely respected leader in many organizations and causes
  devoted to abolition of slavery, bringing progress to the people of Africa and supporting
  Quaker groups in America and England to improve the lot of their fellow man"--
  Provided by publisher.
Identifiers: LCCN 2020043968 | ISBN 9780932027375 (paperback)
Subjects: LCSH: Cuffe, Paul, 1759-1817. | Cuffe, Paul, 1759-1817--Friends and associates. |
  Slocum, Cuffe, approximately 1718-1772. | Cuff family. | Slocum family. | Massachusetts
  --Genealogy. | African American abolitionists--Massachusetts--Biography. |
  Abolitionists--Massachusetts--Biography. | Quakers--Massachusetts--Biography. | Back
  to Africa movement.
Classification: LCC E185.97.C96 C65 2020 | DDC 326/.8092 [B]--dc23
LC record available at https://lccn.loc.gov/2020043968

# Dedication

*We dedicate this book to the memory of Geraldine Millham who devoted much of her life to preserving the history of the Town of Westport, who was always willing to provide a helping hand and spectacular images to embellish any of our projects or publications, and who, most of all, was a dear and wonderful friend.*

# Contents

# Preface

*I* OWE A GREAT debt to Lee Blake, Executive Director of the New Bedford Historical Society, for first drawing my attention to Paul Cuffe and to Carl Cruz, Cuffe descendant and New Bedford resident, for further stimulating my interest by feeding fascinating facts and bits of information about Paul Cuffe and his family to me over the years.

It all started with a symposium called "Paul Cuffe, the Man and His Legacy," which Lee, Betty Slade, and colleagues organized in 2009. I had already read Lamont Thomas's excellent biography of Paul Cuffe and was attracted especially to his descriptions of Cuffe's involvement in Sierra Leone. I wanted to understand what it was that he was trying to achieve in Africa and how it actually worked out. So, I volunteered to write a paper on that subject for the symposium.

My interest in this particular aspect of Paul Cuffe's life was linked to the fact that I had undertaken a somewhat similar endeavor in Africa at almost the same age and stage of my life. My project was in a remote part of Sudan, in East Africa, rather than Sierra Leone, which is in West Africa, and it was some 170 years after Paul Cuffe last visited the continent, meaning I could fly easily from Massachusetts to Africa in a few hours rather than battling Atlantic storms on a small brig for a few months. And, with the help of solar panels and a shortwave radio, I could quickly communicate between Africa and America. Yet, I found some conditions in Sudan to be in many ways still untouched by the modern world.

When I read about the tribal structures and territorial conflicts of Sierra Leone during Paul Cuffe's time, they struck me as quite similar to those I had seen on my African trips. The challenges of trying to figure out which would be the most practicable and promising ways to improve the lives of the local people also seemed similar. I wanted to learn more about how Paul Cuffe had handled those challenges and whether he had been any more successful than my colleagues and I had been.[1] That exploration led to the paper "The Struggle for Respect."

That initial engagement, which focused mainly on Cuffe's later life, led to my desire to learn more about his earlier days, and there I found some conflicting stories coming from his several biographers. Some said that he and his family had struggled to survive by working on a farm on the nearby island of Cuttyhunk. Others said the family had cleared a previously unfarmed property in Dartmouth. There were similar conflicting claims about where Paul Cuffe and his family lived at the end of his life. The National Historic Landmark Register of Individual Properties claimed that Paul Cuffe's farm was at one location on the bank of the East Branch of the Westport River, whereas the local Westport Historical Commission said that property had belonged to the Tripp family at that time, not to Paul Cuffe. The local commission did not, however, say where the Paul Cuffe farm or homestead actually was.

These conflicting stories about specific locations and who owned what when, and what they were doing at those locations, led to the realization that I needed to search through local property records and land-use information to determine the truth, or at least get as close to the truth as possible. Betty Slade and I began our search through the local property records at the New Bedford Registry of Deeds. By great good fortune, we discovered Richard Gifford,, a local resident and descendant of many of the old families in this area, who also proved to be an incredible genealogist and repository of information about who lived where and when in much of old Dartmouth and more recent Westport and Dartmouth. We teamed up with Richard and together produced a second major paper, entitled "New Revelations from Old Deeds" for the next symposium about Paul Cuffe, organized by Lee Blake and others, with the theme "Paul Cuffe: Following in His Footsteps," held in Westport on September 17, 2017, the 200th anniversary of Paul Cuffe's death.

The "Deeds" paper focused on the property holdings of Paul Cuffe; his father, Cuff Slocum; and his brother-in-law, Michael Wainer, along with the prior owners of some of their properties. It definitively demonstrates, we believe, where the farms of all three of these people were located, at which times they owned them, how they were acquired, and how they were used. This detailed paper appears at the end of the collection because it is somewhat heavy reading, but it provides the foundation for many of the stories told in the earlier chapters in this book.

We hope it also will provide the basis for correcting the designation of the so-called "Paul Cuffe Farm" on the National Registry.

As Betty and I worked our way through our Paul Cuffe projects, we concluded that there was an under-appreciation of key individuals who had played extremely important roles in his life and of the contributions they had made toward his success. These included his father, his brother-in-law, Michael Wainer, and his most important business partners, William Rotch Sr. and William Rotch Jr. Several of the chapters seek to fill that gap by drawing strands together into three main themes: papers about Paul Cuffe and his purpose and his partners (Chapters 1-4); papers about his progenitor, Cuff Slocum (chapters 5-7), and a final chapter dealing with the property holdings of Paul Cuffe and his brother-in-law, Michael Wainer.

At some point along the way I became aware of the outstanding talents of another Westport resident, Ray Shaw, and managed to interest him in Paul Cuffe. We traveled to Cuttyhunk to envisage where Paul Cuffe and his family lived; and we employed a drone to create scenes of the Westport River, helping Ray visualize the background in his paintings of Cuffe sailing past the Point on his way to Sierra Leone. Ray also created the maps that illustrate the property holdings along the Acoaxet River. He has added great beauty to this book.

Personally, we have had the good fortune to experience living for several decades in a house built during Paul Cuffe's time (1776) at Westport Point in his hometown. Not only have we sailed around the Westport River and Buzzards Bay, as Cuffe did, but we've also visited Cuttyhunk Island, where he was born, even sailing there from Westport Point in a small catboat. We've also read books about the history and lifestyles of people living in this area during the time that Paul Cuffe and his family lived here. From these experiences, we have, in a sense, imbibed the essence and mental images of these places such as: "this is the harbor of Cuttyhunk where Paul and his siblings grew up"; or "Paul Cuffe's windmill was just up the road, and he undoubtedly rode by our house many times on his way to the boat docks at the end of the road"; or, "this is the river bank where he had his boatyard and his home"; or, "this is the Friends Meeting House that he played a major role in building"; or "this is where Cuff Slocum's farm was, and it now has a solar farm named in his honor." We have "lived" these stories vicariously through researching and writing about them. And often, when we thought we finally had the story right, some new bit of information would pop up, causing us to revisit the story and modify it to accommodate the new insight, which usually came from Carl Cruz, or Lee Blake, or Richard Gifford, who have all been part of living and reliving the Paul Cuffe story.

In connection with the Paul Cuffe symposium of 2017, a committee was formed led by Lee Blake and including Carl Cruz, Richard Gifford, Robert Harding, Jane Loos, Judith Lund, Geraldine Millham, Jenny O'Neill, Betty, and me. In addition to organizing the symposium, the committee established a website, paulcuffe.org, which is maintained by the Westport Historical Society and

*Paul Cuffe sailing across Buzzards Bay in a shallop.*

contains many documents and much new information about Paul Cuffe. Many of the papers included in this volume appeared initially on the Paul Cuffe website and are here consolidated and updated. The committee also mapped out and dedicated a new Captain Paul Cuffe Heritage Trail, which identifies and describes some eleven sites in Westport, Dartmouth, and New Bedford that were important in the life of Paul Cuffe and his family.

Betty and I are deeply grateful to all members of the Paul Cuffe Symposium Committee for their continuing inspiration, stimulation, and assistance in helping us celebrate the lives of these distinguished citizens of color of our hometown.

– David C. Cole
Westport, Massachusetts

Note: Regarding the spelling of names—such as Cuff Slocum, Paul Cuffe, other Cuffes, Sowles, etc., and the names of various places—we use the most common contemporary spellings except when quoting from or referring to an original text or document. In such cases, we use the spelling that appears in the specific text or document.

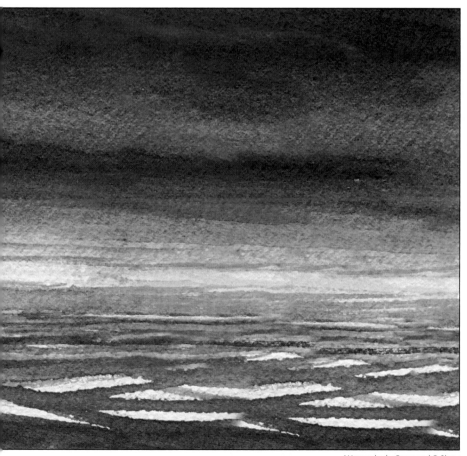

*– Watercolor by Raymond C. Shaw*

# A Brief Biography

*P*AUL CUFFE WAS born on Cuttyhunk Island, at the west end of the Elizabeth Islands chain in Massachusetts, on January 17, 1759. He was the seventh child and fourth son of Cuff Slocum, an emancipated slave from West Africa, and Ruth Moses, a Native American woman from Cape Cod. Cuff and Ruth had ten children, who all lived well into their adult years, a remarkable record for that time.

For about fifteen years, the family lived on Cuttyhunk, where they interacted with Wampanoag neighbors on the Elizabeth Islands and Martha's Vineyard. They were responsible for managing the properties of Holder Slocum at the west end of the Elizabeth Islands that were used mainly for grazing sheep in the warmer months. The Slocums were a well-to-do family who had settled in the mainland town of Dartmouth, Massachusetts.

Paul's parents eventually saved enough of their earnings to purchase an existing 116-acre farm in Dartmouth. The family moved there in the spring of 1767 and lived there together until 1772, when Paul's father died. Cuff Slocum bequeathed this farm to his two younger sons, John and Paul, and it remained in their possession for the next half-century. But in 1773, Paul initiated his seafaring life as a 14-year-old crew member on a voyage to the West Indies, leaving management of the farm to his older brother, John.

*Paul Cuffe as a boy living and tending sheep on Cuttyhunk Island..*

*– Watercolor by Raymond C. Shaw*

Paul again crewed on whaling ships in 1775 and 1776. After being taken prisoner by the British Navy on the latter voyage and held in a jail in New York harbor for three months, Paul took up the challenge of penetrating the British blockade to deliver needed supplies to the residents of Nantucket throughout the rest of the war years. He lost his small boat and supplies to pirates on at least one occasion but succeeded on many crossings in the dark of moonless nights and, in the process, built up relationships with leading families of Nantucket Quakers, such as William Rotch, Sr. and Jr., who became important friends and business partners throughout the rest of his life.

In 1780, Paul, aged 21, and his brother John, 23, joined four free African American friends in petitioning the Massachusetts Legislature to grant them the right to vote. The petition was denied by the House of Representatives but was subsequently incorporated into the State's new constitution, which only required property ownership to qualify men to vote. That same year, Paul and John were jailed for a few days for not paying town taxes on their property as part of their protest to gain the right to vote. But they were rescued by a prominent local citizen, Walter Spooner, who helped negotiate a reasonable settlement.

On February 25, 1783, Paul Cuffe married Alice Abel Pequit, widow of James Pequit and daughter of a prominent Wampanoag family on Martha's Vineyard. They had seven children together, five daughters and two sons, all of whom were born in the Dartmouth/Westport area and lived to maturity. That same year, Paul joined forces with his brother-in-law, Michael Wainer, a Wampanoag who had married his older sister, Mary, in 1772. Paul and Michael established a shipping business that operated across the south coasts of Massachusetts, Rhode Island and Connecticut. In 1789, Paul acquired a small waterfront property on the west bank of the East Branch of the Acoaxet (Westport) River, where he and Michael began building a series of increasingly larger sailing ships that they used to expand their ocean trading business along the East Coast and up into the Canadian Maritime Provinces, for fishing voyages to the Grand Banks, and for whaling voyages throughout the Atlantic Ocean. As Michael and Mary's sons matured, they served as mates, captains, and masters of those ships.

In the latter half of the 1790s, realizing the benefits of their successful trading business, both Paul Cuffe and Michael Wainer established permanent residences for their families on nearby properties along the East Branch. Paul built a substantial house next to his shipyard; Michael Wainer acquired a 100-acre property a quarter-mile to the south, which had been the homestead of the Eddy family and included a sizeable house.

Paul Cuffe became one of the wealthiest persons of color in the United States, and he used his wealth to support local activities and endeavors, such as a smallpox hospital and an integrated school. He also provided aid to many people in need, no matter what their ethnic or racial background. To help with his extensive landholdings and shipbuilding, he partnered with the white community as well as with persons of color in Westport and elsewhere.

As Cuffe expanded his commercial dealings around the Atlantic Ocean, he became increasingly engaged with Quaker businessmen and abolitionist leaders in Baltimore, Philadelphia, New York, and London. The British abolitionists, in particular, saw Paul Cuffe, a prominent black entrepreneur and humanitarian, as a potential ally in their efforts to improve conditions in the colony of Sierra Leone.

This colony had been established in 1791 by England to provide a home for slaves who had sought freedom by taking refuge with British forces during the Revolutionary War. They had been transplanted to Nova Scotia when the British were defeated, and subsequently transported to Sierra Leone in the hope of creating a viable permanent settlement there. This effort had experienced numerous problems. Many settlers had died from tropical illnesses, and there had been continuing conflict between the English commercial and military leaders and the ostensibly free citizens. These problems were compounded when a group of former slaves from Jamaica, referred to as "Maroons," was brought to Sierra Leone in 1800 and injected into this already unstable setting. The situation was further exacerbated after the abolition of slave trading by the British in 1807, which led to the practice of sending any slaves recaptured from illegal British slave-trading ships to Sierra Leone for resettlement.

At the urging of Quakers and abolitionists in England and America, Paul Cuffe sailed to Sierra Leone in 1811 to assess the situation among the various freed-slave communities, British government officials and private traders, and the local African people and to see whether he could suggest ways to improve their conditions. After several months in Sierra Leone, he sailed to England to consult with the leaders of the African Institution, an organization that was committed to promoting commerce and civilization in Africa and providing continuing advice on British colonial policy there. He received a remarkably warm reception from both the Quaker community and the leaders of the African Institution in England.

Choosing Liverpool as his commercial base, Cuffe made two trips to London to pursue various aspects of his Sierra Leone initiatives. He spoke to the members of the African Institution about the potentials he saw for raising export crops and setting up factories and shipyards, similar to those he was familiar with at home, which could be used to process goods for export and build ships for transporting such cargos. Cuffe's recommendations were based on the idea that the Africans, both the returned freed slaves and the local population, would be provided with the assistance needed to initiate and carry out these activities.

While still in England, however, Cuffe discovered that some of the British merchants in Sierra Leone saw his plans as a threat to their protected monopoly positions and had taken measures to undermine his efforts. One of the merchants sent a letter to the African Institution warning them that Paul Cuffe "was an unscrupulous businessman and not to be trusted." The merchants also conspired to have a young man from Sierra Leone, Aaron Richards, forced off Cuffe's ship in Liverpool and held captive, first in Liverpool and then in Portsmouth. Richards was serving as an apprentice to learn navigation with the hope that he might become a skilled mariner and even a future captain of ships sailing out of Sierra Leone. Cuffe tried on his own to get Aaron Richards released in Liverpool. When that failed, he enlisted the support of influential Quakers and leaders of the African Institution, who in turn interceded with the British Admiralty and arranged for Richards' release.

From England, Cuffe and his crew sailed back to Sierra Leone and set about organizing his Nova Scotian friends into a "Friendly Society...that would serve as the catalyst for the development of an African People to be counted among the historians' nations, and it would keep records of its actions to ensure that future historians would be able to reconstruct the story of that nation's rise and progress."

When Cuffe returned to Westport from Sierra Leone in April of 1812, the onset of the war between England and the United States rendered the cargo he was carrying from the British colony of Sierra Leone illegal and the Newport customs officials seized his ship. Undaunted, Paul Cuffe rode the stagecoach to Washington where, through the intercessions of his Quaker friends, he was received by President James Madison (a first for a Black American) and the Secretaries of State and Treasury, who issued orders that his ship and cargo be released. But the war prevented any further involvement with Sierra Leone until after it ended in 1814.

In 1808, Cuffe had been welcomed into membership in the local Meeting of the Quakers in Westport, and its members had strongly supported his Sierra Leone mission. Upon returning home from Sierra Leone and being thwarted by the war from maritime activity, he became more actively involved with the local Meeting. He was appointed to a committee to decide whether a new Meetinghouse building should be constructed and, if so, to oversee and raise the funds for that undertaking. Paul became a leader of that committee and contributed half of the cost of the new building.

After the war with Britain ended, Paul Cuffe led a third trip to Sierra Leone. He transported 10 families, totaling 38 people, on his brig *Traveller*. The agreement with these new settlers was that they would work to assist the local people to become more productive and able to engage in world trade with local commodities, rather than exporting slaves. He had been promised financial support for this venture from the African Institution in London, but that support failed to materialize, and he ended up meeting most of the costs himself. Some of his passengers stayed on in Sierra Leone and some later moved on to the new colony of Liberia, where they reportedly prospered.

A new American organization called the American Colonization Society was being formed about the same time that Paul Cuffe returned from his third trip to Sierra Leone, and its leaders sought his support and endorsement. While its goals of resettling freed slaves in Africa initially seemed consistent with Cuffe's own, it soon became clear to him and other African American leaders that the Society was mainly sponsored by slaveowners who were more interested in removing the free black presence from American society than they were in supporting African development. Cuffe did not give it his support.

Early in the following year, 1817, Paul Cuffe came down with an illness that eventually led to his death on September 7th. He was buried the next day in the cemetery behind the Westport Friends Meetinghouse and was honored and memorialized in many halls and sanctuaries around the Atlantic in the following months.

One of the most eloquent and authoritative of these tributes was by the Reverend Peter Williams Jr, Minister of the African Methodist Episcopal Zion Church in New York City, who had been a close friend of Paul Cuffe for many years. The following excerpts from his discourse give his assessment of him:

> In his person, Captain Cuffee was large and well proportioned. His countenance was serious, but mild. His speech and habit, plain and unostentatious. His deportment, dignified and prepossessing; blending gravity with modesty and sweetness, firmness with gentleness and humility. His whole exterior indicated a man of respectability and piety.
>
> He was so conscientious that he would sooner sacrifice his private interests than engage in any enterprise, however lawful or profitable, that might have a tendency, either directly or indirectly, to injure his fellow men. For instance, he would not deal in ardent spirits, nor in slaves, though he might have done either without violating the laws of his country, and with great prospects of pecuniary gain.
>
> In 1797, Captain Cuffee, lamenting that the place in which he lived, was destitute of a school for the instruction of youth; and anxious that his children should have a more favorable opportunity of obtaining education than he had had, proposed to his neighbours to unite with him in erecting a school-house. This, though the utility of the object was undeniable, was made the cause of so much contention, probably on account of his colour, that he resolved at length to build a school-house on his own land, and at his own expense. He did so, and when finished, gave them the use of it gratis, satisfying himself with seeing it occupied for the purposes contemplated.
>
> As a private man, he was just and upright in all his dealings, an affectionate husband, a kind father, a good neighbor and a faithful friend. Pious without ostentation, and warmly attached to the principles of Quakerism, he manifested, in all his deportment, that he was a true disciple of Jesus; and cherished a charitable disposition to professors of every denomination, who walked according to the leading principles of the gospel.
>
> Captain Cuffee was a judicious and a good man. His thoughts ran deep, and his motives were pure. Such was his reputation for wisdom and integrity, that his neighbours always consulted him in all their important concerns, and, oh! what honor to the son of an African slave, the most respectable men in Great Britain and America were not ashamed to seek to him for counsel and advice!"

# The Struggle for Respect:

## Paul Cuffe and His Nova Scotian Friends in Sierra Leone

*P*AUL CUFFE HAD, over the years, earned the respect and admiration of many of his contemporaries who had come to know him. Leading citizens of New Bedford, Westport, and Providence counted him as their friend and partnered with him in business ventures. But when he ventured out of this circle of acquaintances, he often had to prove his legitimate claim for respect. The well-known story of his encounter with a prejudiced fellow passenger in the stagecoach on his way home from meeting with President Madison and other leading government officials is but one of what must have been an endless number of challenges to his legitimacy and worth as a human being.

Prominent Quakers and abolitionists who knew him, or knew of him, in North America and England, however, sought him out in 1807 to help rescue their troubled effort to establish a viable colony in Sierra Leone that would provide a model for "civilizing" Africa. When he finally traveled to Sierra Leone in 1811 to investigate the possibilities, he found an existing community of "freed slaves" who had been enticed with promises of freedom and respect but who instead had, over a period of two decades, been subjected to mistreatment, broken promises, and outright suppression. Some of their leaders had even been executed as a result of their efforts to achieve their legitimate rights.

Paul Cuffe quickly befriended these African "Nova Scotians," who were actually slaves from America who had gained their freedom during the Revolutionary War, spent eight years in a kind of semi-slavery in Nova Scotia, and then been taken voluntarily to Sierra Leone to populate a new British-sponsored settlement in 1791. Cuffe recognized in them the same yearning for freedom and equality that motivated him, and he sought to collaborate with them in advancing that cause. He also encountered the prejudices and domination of white English officials, merchants, and slave traders who sought to frustrate these efforts and keep the black settlers "in their place."

Cuffe worked with the Nova Scotians to organize a Friendly Society and to draw up a petition that he carried to London to present to British officials in the summer of 1811. In London, he also sought support from the African Institution—a group that was committed "to stimulating trade with Africa, without itself trading, to promote African education and improved farming methods, and to be a watch-dog against the slave trade."[2]

Cuffe was very warmly received in England by both government officials and members of the African Institution. He was granted special rights to trade with Sierra Leone and was encouraged to continue working with the black settlers there. Unfortunately, when he returned to Sierra Leone, the welcome he received from the white English officials and traders there was not nearly as warm;

nonetheless, Cuffe continued his efforts to "buck up" the Nova Scotians. When he returned to the United States, despite some difficulties with local customs agents, Cuffe was applauded for his efforts on behalf of African development and was promised support from many quarters.

Although Cuffe had intended to return to Sierra Leone in 1812 to continue his efforts, war between the United States and Great Britain forced a postponement for four years. When he did return in 1816, taking with him thirty-eight black settlers, he was older and less vigorous. Meanwhile, developments in Sierra Leone had weakened the position of the Nova Scotians, and the British colonial administration had initiated new programs that enhanced white authority. The struggle for equality and respect for the former slaves, initiated by the Nova Scotians and encouraged by Paul Cuffe, was eclipsed by white colonial domination that set the pattern for Africa for the next century and a half.

Several recent studies have greatly enriched our understanding of the early settlement efforts in Sierra Leone.[3] This paper draws upon these studies in order to provide a better understanding of the interaction between Paul Cuffe and the various other groups involved in the Sierra Leone colony. It also attempts to illuminate the struggles Paul Cuffe and the leaders of the Nova Scotians faced in their attempt to improve their condition.

### Some History

Those not familiar with Africa's history may be inclined to think of it as a continent inhabited by primitive tribes largely untouched by the outside world in the early eighteenth century. In fact, European and American ships had been visiting the ports of western Africa since the sixteenth century and had built up trading posts, often managed by westerners or children of interracial relationships. In the early years, the trade had consisted mainly of commodities—timber, ivory, and handicrafts exchanged for manufactured goods. But in the latter seventeenth century, and throughout the eighteenth century, African exports had shifted mainly to humans, who were exchanged for rum and fancy textiles. The slave trade, which was well organized and permeated many interior regions, had become a significant aspect of the local culture, along with the tribal hierarchies that managed it. Thus, there had been much interaction between the local peoples and their tribal leaders along the African Coast, on the one hand, and the western commercial traders, agents, and shippers, on the other, prior to initiation of resettlement efforts in the late eighteenth century. Resettling freed African slaves was a new activity, but it was occurring in places where there had been a long history of slavery-oriented interaction between the native populations and Europeans.

African resettlement was actually an outgrowth of the American Revolutionary War. The British had offered freedom to slaves who would cross over to areas of British control in the rebelling colonies. When the British lost the war, the freed blacks would have faced re-enslavement if they had remained in the United States, so many of them were moved to Nova Scotia or found their way to England, where they often ended up as indigents on the streets of London and other cities. Sierra Leone was seized upon as a suitable space for resettling these displaced persons, and Botany Bay in Australia was selected as a destination for British prisoners who could no longer be shipped to the North American colonies.

The original group of settlers sent from England to Sierra Leone in 1787 included no one who had any prior knowledge of the conditions or the peoples into which they were intended to merge.[4] The first known proponent of this settlement was Henry Smeathman, an amateur botanist who had spent three years along the West African coast, from 1771 to 1774, collecting specimens for a British museum at Kew Gardens.[5] In 1785, Smeathman "had told the Committee investigating a possible convict station in West Africa that convicts (presumably mostly white) would die there at the rate of a hundred a month."[6] The next year, in advising the Committee for the Black Poor in London...[7]

> ...he painted a land of immense fertility, perfectly healthy for those who lived
> temperately, where the soil need only be scratched with a hoe to yield grain in
> abundance, where livestock propagated themselves with a rapidity unknown in
> a cold climate, where a hut provided adequate shelter at all seasons. He stressed
> the commercial advantages of a settlement which would repay initial outlay by
> opening new channels of trade. The Committee were impressed and recommended
> his plan to the Treasury."

Smeathman's recommendation to the Committee to push ahead with a settlement plan for blacks seems to have been based primarily on his hope to resolve personal debt problems rather than the welfare of the settlers. But, according to Fyfe, many African domestic servants, destitute Loyalists, and sailors were sold on the plan and determined to go nowhere else; after all, "a native of Sierra Leone then in London had assured them the people there would receive them joyfully."

The Committee, despite many doubts, acquiesced and proceeded with the plan. Smeathman, in the meantime, had died and was replaced as leader of the expedition by a friend, Joseph Irwin, who had no prior experience or special knowledge of Sierra Leone.[8] The one person who had some relevant knowledge, Olaudah Equiano, a freed West African slave who later published his abolitionist autobiography, *Equiano's Travels*, was first appointed commissary for the trip but was subsequently dismissed because he accused Joseph Irwin of cheating.[9] A black man's word did not equal a white man's.

The leader of the expedition that finally sailed from Portsmouth, England, with 411 passengers on April 8, 1787, was Captain Thomas Bouldon Thompson, a naval officer with no previous experience in Sierra Leone. His instructions were "to take the settlers to Sierra Leone, acquire a settlement from the chiefs, land the stores, and stay in the river to help them as long as provisions and crew's health allowed. If the chiefs refused, he was to go on down the coast till he found some more accommodating."[10]

After Captain Thompson and his fleet of three ships arrived in Sierra Leone in May of 1781, he purchased a twenty-square-mile tract of land from a local Temne chief, and the settlers named it Granville Town after abolitionist Granville Sharp. But before they could build even temporary housing, the rainy season began, washing out any cleared lands and bringing diseases that wiped out 86 immigrants by September. At that point, Captain Thompson departed for home, his crews having remained healthy by staying on board the ships loaded with ample supplies.

Attrition of the settlers continued until in December 1789, when a new Temne chief burned the settlement at Granville Town to the ground in retaliation for the burning of one of his villages by a British naval crew. As Peterson describes it, "the first settlement had become in reality the victim of climate, disease, poor soil, and the political vicissitudes of life constantly threatened on one hand by European ship captains and on the other by the local population."[11] These were all circumstances, or conditions, that might have been anticipated prior to launching the settlement plan.

The second wave of settlers, from Nova Scotia, who arrived in Sierra Leone in March, 1792, was not much better prepared for the vicissitudes that they were to encounter.[12] The leader of the expedition, John Clarkson, an erstwhile naval officer, had never been to Sierra Leone. An ardent abolitionist and brother of Thomas Clarkson, he went to Nova Scotia to meet with prospective settlers and arrange their passage to Sierra Leone. Although he tried to present a balanced picture of the risks and dangers of the venture, the Black Loyalists in Nova Scotia and New Brunswick were so eager to get out from under the semi-slavery to which they were being subjected that they flocked to sign up. Nearly 1,200 boarded the 15 ships that sailed out of Halifax on January 15, 1792.

Before leaving England for Nova Scotia, John Clarkson had discussed with the leaders of the Sierra Leone Company the terms that he might offer to the settlers. Key among them were allotments of land for houses and farms and absence of quit rents on those lands. He had also been led to believe that the Company would send directives to their agents in Sierra Leone to lay out those allotments and assemble tools and materials with which to build shelters. He promised these terms to the potential settlers in Nova Scotia, but the Company failed to come through on any of them.

The Black Loyalists had established strong, religious-based communities in Nova Scotia with charismatic leaders, engaging mostly in exuberant ceremonies that mixed African and Christian elements. Clarkson was very successful in establishing strong ties with these religious leaders, and many of them came to see him as a kind of Moses leading them out of Egypt to the promised land. Their belief in his divine powers was reinforced when, on the long voyage to Sierra Leone, he miraculously recovered from an illness they thought had killed him.

Upon arriving in Sierra Leone, Clarkson received letters from the Directors of the Sierra Leone Company asking him to take on the role of superintendent and stay for some months, if not indefinitely, to get the settlers established. He agreed to do so primarily because of his commitment to help the Nova Scotians get established.[13]

Clarkson stayed on until the end of the year (1792) and accomplished much. He established cordial relations with the local African leaders, thereby reinforcing rights to use the land. By and large, he treated the Nova Scotian settlers with respect and won their admiration and devotion. He also established his authority over the British staff and, despite their many failings, got them to perform their duties at a modest level. He began the process of distributing land, never raising the issue of quit rent. Although many individuals, both white and black, had died during those first nine months, the mood of the community was generally upbeat after surviving the first rainy season and entering the more comfortable dry season.[14]

The fundamental problem was that what Clarkson had done and promised to gain the support of the Nova Scotians and the local African leaders was clearly at cross purposes with what a new set of Sierra Leone Company directors in London wanted. Their objectives were to establish a commercially viable plantation system run by British officials using local Africans as laborers. To the extent that the Nova Scotians were allotted any land for their own production, they should pay quit-rent to the Company.

When Clarkson left Freetown, he promised to return and resume his role as a benevolent head of the community. But upon reaching England, he quickly discovered that the Company directors were displeased with his failure to advance their interests and did not intend to send him back to Sierra Leone. In the meantime, those who had replaced him in directing affairs in Freetown, supposedly on a temporary basis, reversed many of his policies, stopped land distribution, and undermined those vestiges of local authority for the blacks that had carried over from the original settlers.[15]

The third wave of settlers in Sierra Leone was a group called "Maroons." These were former slaves who had escaped from Spanish owners in Jamaica and moved up into the mountains in 1655, when the British displaced the Spanish rulers. The Maroons established their own social and political organization, which resisted outside control for 140 years.[16] They became very skilled guerrilla fighters in order to defend their independence. The British authorities tricked one group of them into surrendering in 1795, then rounded them up and shipped them off to Nova Scotia, where they, too, had a miserable existence for five years. Subsequently, 550 of them agreed to be moved to Sierra Leone. They arrived just in time to help the British authorities there to put down a rebellion by the freed slaves who had been shipped to Freetown in 1792. The Maroons stayed on in Sierra Leone, some of them composing a kind of local militia to support the authorities.

More settlers were brought to Sierra Leone after the British government outlawed its subjects from commanding slave ships across the Atlantic in 1807. The British Navy was charged with enforcing this law, and their crews were rewarded financially when they captured such slave ships and "rescued" the slaves. The "freed" slaves were brought into British colonial ports, such as Freetown, and "apprenticed" as servants and laborers or enlisted into a kind of local militia. The designers of this policy had perhaps anticipated that it would put a stop to the slave trade, which it did not do. Instead, many slave ships were captured, their masters and crew brought before local courts, and their freed passengers absorbed one way or another into the local society. "By the end of 1811 (the year Paul Cuffe first visited Sierra Leone), 1,991 slaves had been captured (recaptured) and deposited in Freetown."[17]

The total population of the Sierra Leone Colony in 1811 consisted of 28 Europeans, 982 Nova Scotians, 807 Maroons and 100 Africans, plus approximately 1,000 recaptured Africans and a military garrison of unknown number, giving an approximate total of 2,900 plus the garrison. Aside from the 100 Africans, who had presumably never been enslaved, the population was one percent European and ninety-nine percent ex-slaves from America and Jamaica, via Nova Scotia, plus the recaptures. This was the mix of non-native peoples that Paul Cuffe confronted on his first trip to Sierra Leone in 1811.

## Issues of Governance

The first Sierra Leone settlers from England in 1787 were sent with the most unrealistic and conflicted rules of governance perhaps ever concocted. Granville Sharp, the prime sponsor of the expedition, had spelled out his plan in a document entitled, *A Short Sketch of Temporary Regulations (Until Better shall be Proposed) for the Intended Settlement on the Grain Coast of Africa near Sierra Leone*. As Peterson states:[18]

> The basis of Sharp's thinking on the subject of a perfect society in West Africa was that natural man could be civilized through reason alone. His scheme for the government of the Province of Freedom, therefore, was intended "for a race of men supposed to be uniformly open to the persuasions of reason."

> The community, which was to be entirely self-governing, was to be divided equally into tithings and hundreds. The tithings were groups of ten families each of which elected annually a leader, the tithingman. Every ten tithingmen elected annually an hundredor, and together the tithingmen and hundredors were to form the necessarily minimal government of the settlement. Their function was primarily to keep order, so in them was vested the judicial power of the province. Such a government was preferred by Sharp because its simplicity guaranteed that all men were capable of understanding and participating in it.

Slavery was prohibited in the Province of Freedom. The economic basis was to be free labor.

Many of the initial settlers sent to Sierra Leone in 1787 were ex-slaves recruited (rounded up) from the streets of London and other English cities. Many were illiterate and had no prior sense of community to bind them together or give some texture to the idealized form of governance that Sharp had conceived. They did, upon arriving in Sierra Leone, organize themselves into the specified groups, but their main concern was simple survival. The English officers who accompanied them provided little leadership or protection and had no interest in implementing Sharp's ideals. After two years, when the colony was attacked and burned by a local tribe, those who could escaped into the bush.

Back in London, the promoters of the colony requested, and were granted, a new charter as the Sierra Leone Company in 1791. They sent an agent, Alexander Falconbridge, who had some previous experience in West Africa, to Sierra Leone, where he was able to collect forty-eight of the former residents of Granville Town and bring them together in a new settlement. He remained there with the settlers for six months, assisting them in planting crops and building shelters.[19] His favorable reports to the Directors of the Sierra Leone Company led them to look for a new group of settlers. Fortuitously, at about this time, Thomas Peters, a leader of the freed blacks in Nova Scotia, arrived in London and met with Granville Sharp. Peters had heard of the settlement in Sierra Leone, and working together with Sharp, he petitioned the government to resettle the black refugees from Nova Scotia in Sierra Leone.[20]

Although the system of governance that Sharp had conceived had not worked with the first group of settlers from England, it did resonate with the second group from Nova Scotia. They were already bound together in strong religious communities led by charismatic pastors. They were also strongly committed to the ideas of freedom and self-governance, which had been so egregiously denied them in the United States and Nova Scotia. John Clarkson encouraged their organization of the tithing and hundredor groups and endeavored to deal with their religious and political leaders in a fair and respectful way.

But Clarkson was unwilling to cede real power to the Nova Scotians, and this led to conflict with Thomas Peters, who saw himself "at the head of the people".[21]

As Pybus describes the situation:

> It was he (Peters) who was elected to go to England to petition the government on their behalf; he had garnered the support of the British government; he had marshaled Nova Scotia's black refugees to emigrate. Yet on arrival in Sierra Leone, Clarkson was appointed governor and Peters was denied any role in the administration of the new settlement. Clarkson's rancorous response (to Peters) was prompted by fear that Peters believed that he, not Clarkson, should have been the appointed governor.

It was not just Peters who sought stronger self-government by the blacks. Clarkson received petitions and letters from various groups indicating "they wanted a greater say in the management of their affairs, and they wanted to have their own elected representatives keep order and resolve disputes."[22] Peters died in the midst of that first rainy season, and Clarkson hoped that his strange notions regarding their rights would die with him, but they did not.

As it turned out, Clarkson was more inclined to respect and provide some accommodation for the settlers' demands for respect and self-rule than any of his successors.[23] After his departure, relations between the succeeding governors (William Dawes, Zachary Macaulay, and Thomas Ludlum) and the settlers deteriorated, culminating in the 1800 revolt. One cause of the tension that led to the revolt was the conflicting pressures from the directors in London to collect quitrents and limit the powers of the settlers who, in turn, were demanding legislative and judicial powers to protect their promised rights and control their own colony. Another was that the Governors found the Nova Scotians "uppity" and their religious ceremonies improper. Several attempts by Anglican ministers to draw them into more proper observances had been rebuffed and the ministers had left the colony. After the revolt, some of Nova Scotian leaders were executed, and others were expelled.

Largely because of these troubles, in 1808 the Sierra Leone Company was dissolved by an act of Parliament; all property in Freetown, as well as all authority in Sierra Leone, was transferred to the Crown, making it Britain's first permanent colony in Africa. The former Sierra Leone Company directors in London, having lost their authority over the colony, regrouped themselves as the Africa Institution, committed to promoting commerce and civilization in Africa and providing continuing advice on British colonial policy there.

The successive governors of the new Colonial administration were caught between the conflicting demands from London to hold down costs on the one hand, and the need to accommodate the rapidly increasing inflow of recaptured slaves on the other. Initially the governors dealt with the situation in accordance with the law by recruiting some of the slaves into military service, sending them elsewhere for training; others were indentured to local citizens, especially the white overlords, thus passing on their maintenance costs. As the absorptive limits of these two outlets were reached, the recaptures were increasingly pushed out into the surrounding hinterlands, where they received minimal help or control from the authorities. They became, or at least were perceived to be, a threat to the lives and property of the older settlers.

An unusual solution to this dilemma was reached over a period of several years. Paul Cuffe had an unexpected hand in it. On his return trip from London to Freetown in 1811, he brought with him a Methodist minister and three Wesleyan schoolmasters to take over direction of Methodist activities in Freetown. The minister soon died, and his replacement was rejected by the Nova Scotian Methodist community. So he and the three other English Methodists set about organizing the so-called Liberated Africans into local communities centered around education and religion. This model was soon taken up by the Church Missionary Society (CMS), an unofficial group of the Church of England, which represented its more evangelical element."[24]

Over the period from 1811-12 to 1816, under both Governors Maxwell and MacCarthy, the Church Missionary Society built up an effective system of local administration among the Liberated Africans. With London's approval, Governor MacCarthy delineated the parishes they lived in and assigned a CMS missionary to each. This system largely relieved the colony government of both the cost and the responsibility for providing services and maintaining order in these communities.[25]

The Nova Scotians, with whom Paul Cuffe was most directly associated on his three trips to Sierra Leone, had been, to a significant extent, marginalized by these developments. They had been beaten back in the rebellion of 1800, and some of their leaders were either executed or forced out of the territory of the colony into the surrounding tribal villages. The Maroons had played an important role in suppressing that rebellion and thereby gained an influential role with the Colony authorities. Finally, the many recaptured slaves were being channeled into new villages with white missionaries taking on the religious, educational, and governance roles in those communities. Thus, the Nova Scotians, who had accounted for the largest segment of the population by far during their first decade

*Paul Cuffe in the brig* Traveller *sailing past Westport Point en route to Sierra Leone.* – Watercolor by Raymond C. Shaw

of settlement in Sierra Leone, had become a much smaller and less influential segment by 1811, twenty-four years after they first arrived. Their expectations of self-rule, or at least of having a significant role in the governance of the colony, had been submerged under white dominance of the colonial administration at the center and the increasing government-sanctioned missionary role in the new rural settlements. White traders also dominated commercial activity.

### Paul Cuffe's Response

When Paul Cuffe arrived in Sierra Leone in March, 1811, he sought to meet first with Governor Columbine, and then contact nearby local tribal chiefs (to whom he gave gifts of religious and historical books), and build relations with the leaders of the Nova Scotian groups.[26] As Sidbury suggests, the Nova Scotians' assessments of the history and current conditions in Sierra Leone were probably quite different from those Cuffe had heard from the Governor.

Cuffe found that white traders were uncooperative and that they offered him low prices for the goods that he had imported. Consequently, he dealt mainly with the Nova Scotians. He clearly identified most closely with the positions of the Nova Scotians, although he criticized them as being "too prone to idleness, too fond of liquor, and too inclined toward (religious) doctrinal disputes."[27] Nevertheless, he worked with their leaders to draw up a petition to the Governor and Parliament, urging that Africans from English colonies and America be encouraged to come to Sierra Leone to engage in agriculture, commercial trade, and whaling.

This petition is interesting on several counts. First, although many of the Nova Scotians had initially engaged in farming, by this time a number of them had taken up commercial activities, often employing local natives, or recaptured slaves to work on their farmlands. By moving into commerce, they were more directly challenging the white traders who had dominated that field from the beginning. The fact that the petition called for opening up trading opportunities for Africans, both those already in Sierra Leone as well as those who might respond to the invitation, was a direct challenge to the white trading community. It is not surprising, therefore, that a representative of the white traders "wrote a scathing denunciation of Cuffe to Zachary Macaulay in London, saying that he had never known a more unprincipled, mercenary individual, that Cuffe was no better than a slave trader."[28]

Despite this message, Paul Cuffe was warmly received in England and given every courtesy by the leaders of the African Institution and government officials. One experience in particular demonstrated his resolve and sense of self-worth to them: When a British Royal Navy ship impressed a young member of his crew, Aaron Richards, in Liverpool, Cuffe proceeded directly to London and, with the help of influential friends, obtained his release.

From England, Cuffe sailed back to Sierra Leone and set about organizing his Nova Scotian friends into a Friendly Society that "would serve as the catalyst for the development of an African People to be counted among the historians' nations, and it would keep records of its actions to ensure that future historians would be able to reconstruct the story of that nation's rise and progress."[29] He also bought a house to serve as a permanent base in Freetown, signing over his power of attorney to Dave Edmonds, the Nova Scotian who had become his most trusted friend in the colony.[30]

In February 1812, Cuffe sailed from Freetown for home "to build the third leg on which his African vision would stand."[31] Here again he encountered a hostile reception when Newport customs agents seized his ship because it was carrying cargo from a British colony, something that had been outlawed during Cuffe's absence. Once more he headed directly to the seat of power, and with help from his respectfulz friends, met with President Madison and the Secretaries of State and Treasury, who released his ship. Sidbury also states that "in Washington he cemented his status as the nation's most prominent man of color."[32]

On his return trip to Westport, Cuffe stopped in several towns along the way, meeting with supporters of the Sierra Leone project, giving talks about the colony, and distributing his *Brief Account of the Settlement and Present Situation of the Colony of Sierra Leone in Africa*. He was attempting to generate both financial support and potential recruits for settlement. He "began organizing voluntary societies in port cities to serve as African American allies of the Friendly Society and as nodes in a mostly black Atlantic commercial system.[33] Another function of these societies was "to screen and recruit people of good character who might want to travel to Sierra Leone."

The War of 1812 with England put a damper on these activities. Initially Cuffe sought permission from Congress to continue trading with Sierra Leone, but this was denied. Most New England states were opposed to the war but southern states supported it, and southern representatives were not inclined to give special permission for a black man to engage in trade with an enemy colony.

After the war ended in 1814, both the American and British governments continued to impose trade restrictions that prevented Cuffe from resuming his efforts to build profitable trading relations among America, Africa, and England. Finally, in December of 1815, he was able to sail from Westport for Freetown on his brig, *Traveller,* with a commercial cargo and thirty-eight men, women, and children of color who had signed on to settle there. They were mainly farmers rather than persons with mechanical or other skills. He was not able to raise funds from the African Institution or other sources to support the cost of these settlers, so Cuffe ended up paying for their travel and an initial stake of supplies himself. He helped them get settled for two months and then sailed home with a cargo of African commodities. The trip was very costly for him financially and perhaps physically.

### Paul Cuffe's Purpose

Sidbury concludes that Paul Cuffe

*worked to bring an African people into being, so that they could participate in the expansion of liberty through commerce and self-determination...Their 'country', or nation-state, was almost surely going to be the Sierra Leone that he foresaw emerging from colonial dependence as an autonomous black polity. It would serve as the crucial base from which blacks would become independent merchants, navigators, and finally legislators, a base from which the next generation of black children would disprove assertions that 'people of coulour are not caperable of business,' by showing that they could perform 'upon a level with our neighbours the white Brother...Two things mattered: a place where freed slaves could live in societies controlled by black people, and the creation of a commercial network 'between America and Africa and between England and Africa,' which would bring back together people separated by slavery and the history of warfare that had prevented them from rising into the community of nations.*[34]

These great hopes, that resonated as strongly in the latter half of the twentieth century as they did in the early nineteenth century, were undercut in Sierra Leone at that time by the continued dominance of a white-led colonial government, white traders, white missionaries who organized the resettlement villages, and the exclusion of blacks in their own "country" from the positions of responsibility and respect that had been so easily promised to them by well-meaning benefactors as inducements to get them back to Africa.

# Special Relationships
## With the Rotch and Wainer Families

*P*AUL CUFFE EVOLVED from an unschooled child living within the Wampanoag community on the south coast of Massachusetts into a charismatic and inspirational leader widely known and respected on both sides of the Atlantic. He was born on the island of Cuttyhunk in 1759, the son of a freed slave and a Native American woman. He was largely self-educated but attained a high level of literacy. He learned other skills, such as navigation and shipbuilding, through on-the-job experience. Within the short lifespan of fifty-eight years, Paul Cuffe became a highly respected leader in many organizations and causes, especially those devoted to abolishing slavery and bringing progress to the people of Africa; he also actively supported Quaker groups in America and England working to improve the lot of their fellow man.

Throughout his life, he built powerful relationships with key people in America, England, and Africa who would be most helpful in advancing the causes to which he was committed. Two of the most important of these relationships were with very different families living and working in southeastern Massachusetts: the Rotches, a prominent and wealthy Quaker family of Nantucket and New Bedford, and the Wainers, a humble Native American and African American family of Dartmouth and Westport.

### The Rotches

We do not know exactly when Paul Cuffe first met members of the Rotch family, but it probably was when he was still a teenager. The fact that William Rotch Jr. was born in the same year as Paul Cuffe supports the likelihood of their early relationship. In any case, he developed an extremely close and multifaceted relationship with the Rotch family that lasted well beyond his death.

The Rotches were among the most prominent families of Nantucket before and during the Revolutionary War and in New Bedford, where they moved their base of operations, after the war. In addition to being well-respected members of the Quaker community, they were leaders in the whaling industry and ran successful financial and coastal trading businesses. The intimate relationship between Paul and William Rotch Sr. and William Rotch Jr. over some forty years provides a powerful example of a sincere, unprejudiced, honorable friendship in that era of black slavery and native suppression.

Paul Cuffe crewed on whaling ships in 1773, 1775, and 1776. We do not know whether he crewed on any of the Rotches' whaling ships, but he may well have. In 1775, fifty-eight whaling ships sailed out of Nantucket, more than from any other town in North America. In 1776, the whaling ship on which Paul Cuffe sailed was captured by the British Navy and taken to Brooklyn, New York, where he and the other crew members were held captive on a prison ship for three months. After his release, Paul returned to his family home in Massachusetts. Around that time, he learned about the British Naval blockade of Nantucket and other offshore islands and that their inhabitants were in need of supplies.

Leonard B. Ellis quotes William Rotch Sr.'s description of the difficulties his ships encountered while trying to get supplies to the island (p. 2 of the biographical sketches):

> From the year 1775 to the end of the war we were in continual embarassments (sic). Our vessels were captured by the English, and we were sometimes in danger of being starved. The exposed situation of the islands made it extremely difficult to elude the numerous cruisers that were always in the vicinity, and months would frequently elapse before any supplies could be obtained from the main land.

Paul Cuffe, being aware of this problem for the people of Nantucket, undertook to acquire a small sailing vessel that he used to deliver goods to their island home. This required navigating through the natural hazards of Buzzards Bay and Nantucket Sound while avoiding the British blockade and numerous pirate ships along the way.

According to Daniel Ricketson's *History of New Bedford*, published in 1858, Paul Cuffe, at the age of about twenty: (p. 257)

> undertook a trip to Nantucket with a boatload of produce, but in crossing Buzzards Bay was seized by "refugee pirates," who robbed him of his boat and cargo. Nothing daunted, in connection with his brother,...they built another boat; and having procured a cargo upon his credit, Paul again started for Nantucket, and was again chased by pirates; but night coming, he escaped from them, but ran his boat upon a rock on one of the Elizabeth Islands, and so badly injured her as to render it necessary for him to return to his home on the Westport River. After having repaired his boat, he again set off for Nantucket, reaching there in safety this time, and disposed of his cargo to good advantage. On a subsequent voyage, however, he was again taken by the pirates, and deprived of all except his boat. Still he continued his trips to Nantucket until he had acquired enough to look for a more lucrative business.

Given the prominence of the Rotch family on Nantucket during the War, it seems reasonable to speculate that they were engaged with Paul Cuffe in his Nantucket ventures, especially if he had previously been aboard one of their whaling ships. They may have even helped Cuffe obtain the use of a boat and financed his purchases of goods to bring to them.

After the war, when Paul Cuffe entered the coastal shipping business, he continued to utilize the services of the Rotch family in conducting his financial affairs. There are stories in Ricketson's book (p. 255) of how Paul Cuffe, when he was denied a seat at a table in the main room of a tavern in New Bedford, informed the innkeeper that he was on his way to dinner at the Rotch home. Another story from Ricketson tells about a time when William Rotch Sr. was invited to dinner at the home of Paul Cuffe and his wife, Alice, after attending a gathering at the Friends Meetinghouse in Westport. Upon seeing that there were no places set at the table for Paul and Alice, he refused to sit at that table until the host and hostess joined them. These are just a few examples of the respect and friendship that the Rotches Sr. and Jr. expressed for Paul Cuffe and his family.

As Paul Cuffe expanded his shipping businesses across the Atlantic Ocean, he continued to rely on the Rotches for their financial services and their personal connections. There is much correspondence, easily accessible in Rosalind Wiggins' book, that records such exchanges between Paul Cuffe and William Rotch Jr. and with Rotch Jr.'s brother-in-law, Samuel R. Fisher, a merchant in Philadelphia who handled several business matters for Paul Cuffe.

Another possible connection between Paul Cuffe and the Rotches relates to the British colony of Sierra Leone. After the war, the British government was trying to deal with the many destitute blacks who were found in the streets of London and other major cities. As discussed in the previous chapter, in 1786 the British government decided to establish a kind of colony in Sierra Leone and to resettle those black individuals and families there who would be willing to go. This policy was strongly debated in the newspapers. Many of the formerly enslaved black people who had been enticed onto ships at Gravesend found that they were being held captive and claimed that their lives were as bad as they had been on slave ships.

That same year, William Rotch Sr. visited London in an effort to gain British government support for a scheme to transfer what remained of the Nantucket whaling fleet to England to resume their whaling activities. The British initially rejected his proposals, and he went on to Paris, where he received a much warmer reception. But during the time that he was in London, he became aware of the deliberations relating to resettlement of free black people in Sierra Leone, and according to Wiggins (p. 265), he discussed these matters with Granville Sharp and William Dillwyn, leading Quakers and abolitionists in London. Wiggins notes that Rotch undoubtedly reported on these issues to the Quaker community in New England when he returned home in 1791. He also probably spoke about it with his business partner, Paul Cuffe, thereby sparking an idea in Paul's mind some two decades before he would ever set sail for Sierra Leone.

Perhaps the ultimate confirmation of the close relationship between Paul Cuffe and William Rotch Jr. is to be found in the latter's role at the end of Paul's life in September, 1817. For one thing, William Rotch Jr. was appointed the executor of Paul Cuffe's will. He also delivered a eulogy at Paul's funeral and may have been the author of his death notice in the New Bedford *Mercury*. The settlement of Paul Cuffe's estate proved to be so complicated that it took most of the next decade for his friend to complete the process. But that was not the end of the relationship.

William Rotch Jr. probably arranged for the preservation of many Cuffe documents, then passed them along to his brother-in-law, Samuel Rowland Fisher, a prominent Quaker Merchant in Philadelphia and friend of Paul Cuffe. Fisher's descendants preserved them for more than a century before turning them over to the New Bedford Free Public Library in 1943. The collection included many of Paul Cuffe's papers, ship logs, and other documents, totaling 1,250 pages. The source of these documents, as given in its Accession Report, was as follows:

*The collection of papers of the Cuffe family, including Paul Cuffe, John Cuffe and Cuffe Slocum, were originally compiled by Samuel R. Fisher of Philadelphia, PA, brother-in-law of William Rotch Jr. of New Bedford, MA. Fisher was the great-grandfather of Anna Wharton Wood, who ultimately donated the documents to the New Bedford Free Public Library.*

The line of genealogical relationships, and possibly of transmission, is as follows:

- William Rotch Jr. married Elizabeth Rodman in 1782
- Hannah Rodman, sister of Elizabeth Rodman, married Samuel Rowland Fisher (1793)
- Deborah Fisher (1795-1888), daughter of Samuel and Hannah Fisher, married William Wharton (1795-1856) in 1817
- Hetty F. (alias Esther) Wharton (1836-1915), daughter of William and Deborah Wharton, married Benjamin R. Smith in 1859
- Anna Wharton Smith (1864-1945), daughter of Benjamin R. and Esther Smith, married Henry Austin Wood (1855-1942) in 1898; they lived in Waltham, MA
- Anna Wharton Smith Wood gave the Cuffe papers to the New Bedford Free Public Library on October 23, 1943

The documents, which have been preserved by the New Bedford Free Public Library, have proven a rich source for research by many who have sought to gain a better understanding and appreciation of Paul Cuffe.

William Rotch Jr.'s preservation of these documents has thus proven to be a remarkable act of honor and respect for a dear friend and a great man. Thanks to the conservation efforts of the Fisher descendants and the New Bedford Free Public Library, the legacy of Paul Cuffe lives on.

## The Wainers

Paul Cuffe's relationship with Michael Wainer and his family proved extremely important, much as his relationship with the Rotch family did. However, the ancestry of Michael Wainer and the nature of Paul Cuffe's relationship with him and his family were markedly different from that which he had with the Rotches. Michael Wainer, named Micah Quebbin at birth in 1748, was the son of a Wampanoag woman, Mary Quebbin, and lived his early years in a Native community on either Martha's Vineyard or in Dartmouth, or both. He had no formal education and apparently never learned to write, as he still signed deeds late in life with his mark rather than a signature. While Paul and Michael were living within a few miles of each other and may have known each other beforehand, the relationship undoubtedly got a strong boost when Michael married Paul's older sister, Mary, in 1772, a few months after Paul and Mary's father, Cuff Slocum, died.

Michael Wainer probably crewed on whaling ships out of Nantucket or Dartmouth in his teen years, but it's likely that he also worked as an assistant or apprentice to some tanners in the Russells Mills section of Dartmouth because he became sufficiently skilled to set up a tanning and shoemaking business on a property he purchased in the same area in 1776. There is no record of when he changed his name from Quebbin to Wainer, but it is conceivable that he took the name Wainer as a shortened form of "cordwainer," which was the common name of a person engaged in the shoemaking craft that he was practicing.

Michael Wainer may well have been like an older brother to Paul Cuffe and probably helped him get hired as a crew member on whaling ships when he was only fourteen years old. He may also have employed Paul in his tanning operations. There is no evidence that Michael was involved in Paul's Nantucket supply runs during the Revolutionary War, but he may well have helped Paul launch his coastal shipping business after the war.

After Paul bought a small property on the west bank of the East Branch of the Acoaxet (Westport) River and set up a shipyard there in 1789, Michael became an active partner in the business. Within two years, Michael and Mary sold their property and tanning business at Russells Mills and bought some farmland nearer the shipyard. Michael and Paul would go on to become owners and captains of the increasingly larger sailing ships built at that shipyard.

One of the most important links between Paul Cuffe and the Wainers was the fact that Michael and Mary Wainer had seven sons, and all of them sailed on and commanded the ships that were built and owned by their Uncle Paul and their father. Three of them—Thomas, John, and Michael—sailed with their Uncle Paul on his first trip to Sierra Leone in 1811.

Another manifestation of the close relationship between Paul Cuffe and the Wainers occurred in the years 1799 and 1800. Ebenezer Eddy, who had inherited much of his father's property along the west bank of the East Branch of the Acoaxet River, wanted to sell two large parcels. They were the hundred-acre Eddy family homestead and a forty-acre farm field known as the "Allen Lot." Paul Cuffe purchased these two properties from Ebenezer Eddy in March of 1799, the homestead for $2,500 and the farm lot for $1,000. It is clear that he bought the Eddy homestead not for himself, but for his sister and brother-in-law, Mary and Michael Wainer, and their family because Paul transferred ownership of the Eddy homestead to Michael and Mary the following year, and the deed indicates that the Wainers had already been living on that property. Paul, meanwhile, retained the "Allen Lot," later willing it to his youngest son, William Cuffe.

There are logical explanations for this two-stage transfer of the Eddy homestead. Paul Cuffe had recently built a sizeable new home, valued at $600 in a 1798 property tax assessment, on his shipyard property, and he was probably comfortably settled with his family in that new home. Meanwhile, just two months before Paul bought the Eddy homestead, Michael Wainer had spent $600 to purchase a twenty-four-acre farm property, which probably had a house on it, on Hix Bridge Road. The purchase may have left him with insufficient funds to buy the Eddy homestead, so his brother-in-law, Paul Cuffe, put up the money and put his name on the deed.

The Eddy homestead was a much more favorable location than the Hix Bridge Road property. It was closer to the Paul Cuffe residence and docks, and the house on it was most likely much larger and more suitable for them than the one that the Wainers had just purchased. It was probably a joint decision of Paul and Michael to buy the Eddy property and move the Wainers into that residence. When Michael did repay Paul the original $2,500 purchase amount a year later, he concurrently sold the Hix Bridge property to his oldest son, Thomas, thereby raising a part of the money needed for the new transaction.

Mary Wainer, Michael's wife and Paul Cuffe's sister, died in December of 1804. Two months later their son, Jeremiah Wainer died from injuries suffered at sea while commanding the Cuffe-Wainer ship *Ranger*. These two tragedies at the core of the two families must surely have drawn them even closer together. Michael, who was eleven years older than Paul, seems to have largely given up his sailing voyages by this time and was spending most of his time at home. Having taken on an apprentice cordwainer, Henry Peters, shortly after he moved to his new homestead, he was undoubtedly active in this trade and busy instructing and supervising his new employee. But he probably still visited the shipyard and the nearby Cuffe family home on a regular basis.

One final testimony to the close relationship between Paul Cuffe and Michael Wainer is that Michael, when he drew up his will in 1814, designated Paul Cuffe, along with his eldest son, Thomas, and his immediate neighbor, Tillinghast Tripp, as the executors of his will. The fact that Paul Cuffe made his final long trip to Sierra Leone shortly after Michael's death, and then became ill and died within a few months after his return, meant that the burden of executor fell mainly on the other two designees.

### Summing Up

In one sense, the Rotches provided Paul Cuffe with strong connections to the outside world—to the Quaker community, the abolitionist community, the financial and business world, and to the upper echelons of the English, European, and American societies. The Wainers, on the other hand, helped Paul Cuffe build his connections with the Native American community and the seamen and workers along the south coast of Massachusetts. These two sets of relationships began when Paul was a teenager and lasted throughout his life. Mutual respect and great affection were manifest in both. Ultimately, his relationships with the Rotches and Wainers helped Cuffe realize his full potential and achieve great respect in a world that was rife with prejudice, suppression, and disrespect for persons of his heritage.

# Selected Transcriptions:
## From the Westport Friends Monthly Meetings

*T*HE FOLLOWING TRANSCRIPTIONS are from the minutes of the Men's Meetings of the Westport Society of Friends. They include all of the entries relating to Paul Cuffe for the period from 1808, when he became a member of that Meeting, until his death in 1817. The minutes clearly demonstrate the respect in which he was held and the support he was given by this group. An interesting fact that links this chapter and the previous chapter is that Gardner Wainer, Paul Cuffe's nephew, and Rhoda, Paul Cuffe's niece, were admitted to the Dartmouth Friends Meeting in 1810.

### Requesting and being received into membership in the Society:

**1808 2nd month.** *Inform that Paul Cuffe requests to come under the care of friends, We therefore appoint Jeremiah Austen, Prince Wing, and Abner Potter to visit him and take a solid opertunity with him in order to discover the motive and sincerity of his request and fitness to become a member of our Society and report to next meeting. (p. 111)*

**1808 4th month.** *The committee in the case of Paul Cuffe's request reported that they have had several opportunities with him and he appeared to them to be sincere in what he has requested, therefore after considering thereon we do with the concurrence of the Women's meeting receive the said Paul Cuffe under our care as a member of the society, of which Prince Wing is to inform him. (p. 114)*

### Receiving support from the Society for his first voyage to Africa:

**1810 9th month.** *Our friend Paul Cuffe informs this meeting that he had thoughts of making a voyage or visit to Africa if his friends had unity with his prospect – We therefore appoint John Mosher, Abner Potter, Benjamin Davol, Philip Dunham, Joseph Tripp and Resolved Howland to advise with Paul in the subject and report to next monthly meeting. (p.143)*

**1810 10th month.** *The committee to advise with Paul Cuffe respecting his prospect of making a voyage to Africa report that they had attended to their appointment and left him at liberty to pursue his prospect as way may open, and presented a few lines as a letter of recommendation which being read was approved herein and signed by the Clerk and is as followeth—*

*From the Monthly Meeting of the religious society of friends called Quakers, held in Westport in the State of Massachusetts, United States of America the 13th day of the 10th month, 1810:*

*Our friend Paul Cuffe having informed us that he has some prospect of making a voyage to Africa, we hereby certify that he is a member of our Society and a man whose orderly life and careful conduct has recommended him to the esteem of his friends, desiring that he may experience divine preservation in his present undertaking, we recommend him to the friendly attention and assistance of all well-disposed people where his lot may be cast. Signed by direction and on behalf of said meeting. Ebenezer Baker, Clerk (p. 145)*

### Evaluating sincerity and fitness of new applicant members in the Society:

**1812 9th month.** *Westport meeting informed that Humphry Eldredge requested to be admitted a member of our Society, after considering thereon, we appoint David Tripp, Paul Cuffe and Prince Wing to visit him and endeavor to enquire into his sincerity and fitness to become a member and report to a future meeting. (p. 168)*

**1812 11th month.** *The committee that was appointed to visit Humphrey Eldridge reported that they believe him to be convinced of friend's principles and his endeavoring to support them after considering thereon this meeting received him as a member of our Society and Jeremiah Austin is appointed to inform him thereof. (p. 168)*

### Deciding on the need for a new meeting house and arranging construction:

**1813 1st month.** *The situation of this meeting house coming before us at this time, after Prince Wing, Ebenezer Baker and Paul Cuffe to take it into consideration and see what alteration would be best reflecting it and estimate the cost and report to next monthly meeting. (p. 170)*

Westport Quaker Meeting House and Paul Cuffe Monument.

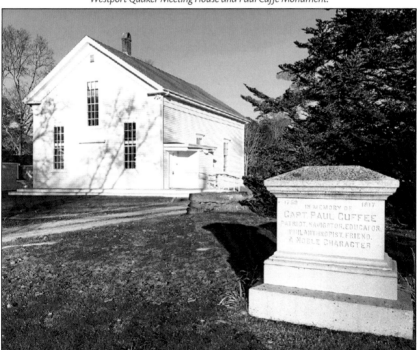

– Photograph by David C. Cole

**1813 2nd month**. *The committee to view and examine the old meeting house in order to ascertain whether it may be best to repair it or build a new one, report in favor of building a new house to take down the high part of the house and let the lower part stand to hold meetings in while the new house is in building the new house to be forty-five feet by thirty with galerys with sliders for the accomodations of mens and womens meetings to be held spate much in the form meeting houses are generally built with a portch fourteen feet by ten. The committee find that a new house of the above description can be got built for twelve hundred dollars with working in what stuff that may be utilizable from it out of that part taking down. After deliberate consideration thereon we unite therewith. Paul Cuffe and Ebenezer Baker is appointed to have the care of cutting some of the principle xxxxxx for the meeting house.*

*We appointed Isaac Peckham, Joseph Tripp, Samuel Hewitt, Ebenezer Baker and Charles Baker to put out subscriptions for the purpose of building a new meeting house.*

**1813 4th month**. *Representatives that were appointed to the Quarterly meeting reported that the Quarterly meeting united with the proposition that this meeting sent to them respecting building a new meeting house and ordered their treasurer to pay this meeting four hundred dollars when the building is completed. (p. 172)*

*This meeting concludes to build a new meeting house forty-five feet by thirty with a portch fourteen feet by ten, and we appointed Paul Cuffe, Ebenezer Baker, Prince Wing, Abner Potter, Joseph Tripp, George Brightman and Samuel Hewitt to superintend the said building and see that it is completed and report when done. (p. 173)*

**1813 8th month**. *The committee that was appointed to have the care of building the new meeting house are authorized by this meeting to call on our treasury for money that may be needed for the purpose of the said house and he to pay the same as far as he is able. (p. 176)*

## Receiving support from the Society for his second voyage to Africa:

**1813 11th month**. *Our esteemed friend Paul Cuffe informed this meeting that he had a prospect of going to the city of Washington on business of importance and requests a few lines setting forth his right of membership among friends, he being a member of our Society and this meeting unites with him in the said prospect and the clerk is directed to give him a copy of this minute. (p. 179)*

**1814 3rd month**. *The committee appointed in the fourth month last to superintend the building of the meeting house in Westport reported at this time that the House was finished and the cost had amounted to eleven hundred and ninety-eight dollars and the committee is dismissed. Our friend Paul Cuffe returned a copy of a minute granted him in the 11th month last. (p. 181)*

**1815 11th month**. *The copy of a minute granted to our friend Paul Cuffe being returned, the following recommendation is approved of and signed by the Clerk. Our friend Paul Cuffe who is a member of our religious society informed this meeting that he has a prospect of making a voyage to Africa on business and in a particular manner, with the laudable view of endeavoring to promote the temporal* and civil improvement and comfort of the inhabitance of some parts of that country which having had our solid deliberation, we feel desirous that he may be enabled to accomplish his object to the peace of his own mind, and leave him at liberty to pursue his prospect, recommending him to the friendly notis and regard of those among whom his lot may be cast.

*Signed by direction and on behalf of our monthly meeting of the religious society of Friends held in Westport, State of Mass. The 16th of the 11th month, 1815, by Ebenezer Baker, Clerk, (p. 199)*

### Final records of his return from Africa and his passing:

**1816 7th month.** *Paul Cuffe returned a letter of recommendation granted to him in the 11th month last when he went on his voyage to Africa. (p. 206)*

**Acoaxett Monthly Meeting: Births, Deaths and Marriages, 1766-1882.** *"Our friend Paul Cuffe was born the 17th of the first month 1759 and departed this life the 7th day of the 9th month 1817 and was buried the 8th of the same month in Friends Burying Ground at Acoaxxet Meeting House. (p. 61)*

# The Remarkable Story of Cuff Slocum

$C$ UFF SLOCUM, UNTIL now, has been known for essentially one thing— being the father of Paul Cuffe. This has earned him a few lines in articles about his famous son and a few pages in the more extended biographies of Paul Cuffe. These publications note that he had been brought to New England as a young slave, gained his freedom somehow, married a Native American woman, and together with her, conceived and raised ten children, one of whom was Paul Cuffe.

This chapter represents a first attempt to delve more deeply into various available sources of information— some old and some new— in order to present a more complete and accurate story of Cuff Slocum. We seek to demonstrate why he should receive much greater recognition for his remarkable accomplishments. In many respects, he provided a launching pad for his son Paul and his daughter Mary. Mary married Michael Wainer, Paul Cuffe's long-term friend and business partner, and Mary and Michael had five sons who became captains on Cuffe/Wainer ships.

Essentially nothing is known about Cuff Slocum's early life in Africa, except that his given name (a version of the name Kofi) indicates that he was from the Ashanti area of West Africa, and that he was brought to Newport, RI on a slave ship. But information on what happened after he arrived in North America, although still limited, has some solid foundations. Three deeds and a will provide critical reference points for his story, but there is much more to be gleaned from his own records, the records of those with whom he interacted, and various studies that give insight into the conditions of the times and places in which he lived. All of these provide us with a fascinating and inspiring story.

The first recorded document about Cuff Slocum is the 1742 bill of sale transferring his ownership as a slave from Ebenezer Slocum to John Slocum. The next records are the registration of his intentions to marry Ruth Moses in 1746 and their actual marriage in 1747. The Dartmouth Vital Records document the birth of their first child, David, in 1747 in Dartmouth, but there are no official records beyond that. Family records, however, show the rest of their nine children born between 1748 and 1766 but do not indicate where those births occurred. Other evidence suggests that the second son, Jonathan, was born in Dartmouth and that the other eight children were born on Cuttyhunk Island.

A deed from the office of the Town Clerk of Glocester, Rhode Island, records that in 1762, Cuff and Ruth purchased a 156-acre property in northwest Rhode Island from Nicholas Lapham of Dartmouth, Massachusetts. Another deed registered in Bristol County, Massachusetts, in 1766 records the purchase of a 120-acre farm in Dartmouth from David Brownell, also of Dartmouth. Then there is Cuff Slocum's will, in which he declares that John Slocum set him free. He therein bequeaths his Glocester property to his two older sons, David and Jonathan, and his Dartmouth farm to his two younger sons, John and Paul.

There are three other important sources of information about Cuff Slocum. The first is a mention of him in the first biography about his son Paul Cuffe written in 1807.[35] The second is an Exercise Book that belonged to Cuff Slocum in which he and others made notes and scribbles about events in his life and those of his family.[36] The third item is a statement written in 1851 by Ruth Cuffe, daughter of David Cuffe, that records a story she had heard a half-century before; the statement describes the circumstances surrounding her grandfather's gaining his freedom and of his later marriage to Ruth Moses.[37] Then there are more recent publications that provide information on the conditions of the times and places where Cuff Slocum and his family lived, which provide useful background and supplements to this story.

### The Deed of Sale and Becoming a Free Man

The deed of sale entered into between Ebenezer Slocum and his nephew John Slocum on February 17, 1742 in the town of Dartmouth transferred the ownership of "a certain negro man of about twenty-five years of age named Cuffe" from Ebenezer to John Slocum for a price of £150.[38] This deed provides no indication of John Slocum's intentions with regard to the negro man named Cuffe, but there is strong evidence that, within a few years, John Slocum granted Cuffe his freedom.

There is a statement at the beginning of Cuff Slocum's will that reads, "I Cuf Slocum formerly a cervant of John Slocum and thence by him sett free and now a free man." While this makes clear that it was John Slocum who freed him, it does not provide a date for when this occurred or what were the steps that led to his freedom.

Our hypothesis is that John Slocum attributed earnings or value of work to Cuff at a rate of £50 per year, which would match his purchase price after three years. This would be consistent with the following statement by his granddaughter, Ruth Cuffe: "[W]hen grandfather Cuffe had worked long enough to pay for himself then his master freed him."

Ruth's narrative supports the following conclusions about the freeing of Cuff Slocum:

- At the time of Cuff's purchase in 1742, his new owner, John Slocum, purchased Cuff with the intention of freeing him after he had worked for a sufficient period of time to, in effect, pay off his purchase price. There is no record of what this rate of payment was or when the period started and ended, but given that Cuff was purchased in February of 1742, and that he took actions, mentioned below, indicating that he was a free man in 1745, it seems reasonable to conclude that he worked off his purchase price over a period of three years at a rate of £50 per year.

- The identity of the "squire" who drew up a paper recognizing Cuff's freedom is not known for sure, but it appears to be a cousin of John Slocum by the name of Holder Slocum. Captain Holder Slocum owned a large homestead farm in Dartmouth at that time and in 1751 acquired possession of the three western islands of the Elizabeth Island chain—Pasque, Nashawena, and Cuttyhunk.

As described below, Cuff Slocum and his family worked for Holder Slocum on Cuttyhunk for an extended period. It seems reasonable, then, to assume that Holder was the one who drew up the paper granting Cuff his freedom and then immediately hired him.[39]

- According to Ruth Cuffe's testimony, his former owner, John Slocum, advised Cuff at the time of his becoming a free man, "to live a steady life and to take good care of his money that he was going to work for and save it so as to get him a home sometime or other." As described below, Cuff took that advice to heart.

*The Deed of Sale of Cuff Slocum*

### Marriage of Cuff Slocum and Ruth Moses

On January 31, 1745, intentions of marriage between Cuffe Slocum and Ruth Moses, both of Dartmouth, were entered with the Town Clerk of Dartmouth, Benjamin Akin.[40] On July 7, 1747, Cuffe(e) Slocum, a negro man, and Ruth Moses, an Indian woman, both of Dartmouth, were married by Phillip Taber, a minister in Dartmouth.[41]

While the dates of the births of Cuff and Ruth Slocum's children are clear from various family records, the locations of their births are less certain. The first son, David, is reported to have been born in Dartmouth on November 15, 1747.[42] Jonathan is believed to have also been born in Dartmouth, on November 12, 1748; their third child, Sarah, is believed to have been born February 5, 1751, on Cuttyhunk. The records indicate that the family moved from Dartmouth to Cuttyhunk Island, the most westerly of the Elizabeth Islands, between 1748 and 1751. Their next seven children, including son Paul Cuffe, were all believed to have been born on Cuttyhunk between 1753 and 1766.[43]

### Living on Cuttyhunk

Cuff and Ruth Slocum and their growing family lived on the island of Cuttyhunk, off the southeastern coast of mainland Massachusetts, from sometime in 1750-51 to the spring of 1767, when they moved to a newly purchased farm "on the main" in Dartmouth. An obvious question arises as to what they were doing on Cuttyhunk. Earlier biographers have suggested that they had a farm and were growing crops for themselves and for sale, or that they moved to Chilmark on Martha's Vineyard, where Cuff was doing various odd jobs.[44]

After reviewing the literature about the history of Cuttyhunk and the other Elizabeth Islands, and more broadly on rural life in New England in the mid-eighteenth century, we have concluded that they were mainly engaged in looking after flocks of sheep (and some other livestock) that were brought from Dartmouth to these western Elizabeth Islands for grazing from mid-spring to mid-fall from various farms in Dartmouth.[45]

They either built a small house or moved into an existing house on Cuttyhunk. They probably had a small garden for raising their own food and fiber. Cuff, subsequently joined by his sons, spent the days looking after the livestock during the milder months, and would have fished, hunted game, and harvested firewood during the winter. His wife, Ruth, subsequently joined by her daughters, tended the garden, prepared the food, and spun both wool and flax into yarn and clothing and looked after the younger children.

As mentioned previously, Holder Slocum acquired the western Elizabeth Islands in 1751, about the same time that the Cuff Slocum family moved to Cuttyhunk, so Cuff and his family would have been working for Holder Slocum. They were probably not only taking care of his livestock but also that of his relatives and neighboring farmers in Dartmouth, who paid him for such grazing rights. Supporting this theory is the record that Holder's son, Christopher Slocum, after the death of his mother, Rebecca Slocum, in 1773, levied a charge of £60 on her estate for grazing 284 sheep on Cuttyhunk for three years.[46]

*Cuff Slocum's home overlooking the harbor on Cuttyhunk Island. – Watercolor by Raymond C. Shaw*

Cuff Slocum's Exercise Book and Book of Accounts found in Paul Cuffe's papers contain a record indicating that he and one of his sons, probably David, the eldest, also worked on helping to build a house on Cuttyhunk for Rebecca Slocum in 1764. They were each paid 3 shillings per day for this work. This fact provides an indicator of the going rate of compensation for them. If we assume that Cuff was credited for working six days a week for 52 weeks per year for Holder Slocum at 3 shillings per day, this would translate into £47 and 8 shillings per year, which can be rounded up to £50 per year.

Over the period of sixteen years from 1751 to 1767 that he was living and working on Cuttyhunk, Cuff Slocum might have earned a total of about £800. Since living expenses were presumably not very great, as the family probably produced most of their own food and clothing and did not have to pay for their housing, these earnings provided the funds with which Cuff and Ruth Slocum purchased two large farms on the mainland in the 1760s.

### Purchasing Two Large Properties

In 1762, Cuff Slocum purchased a 156-acre property in the village of Glocester in the northwest corner of Rhode Island for £90 from Nicholas Lapham, a resident of Dartmouth, Massachusetts.[47] This property was some forty miles from his subsequent farm in Dartmouth, as the crow flies, and a much longer journey by pathways on horseback or foot. It is not clear why Cuff Slocum purchased this property. Perhaps he just wanted to be a property owner, and this was a relatively low price for land. It appears that Cuff never engaged in any farming or woodcutting activities on this property and he may never even have visited it.

In his will, Cuff bequeathed the Glocester property to his two older sons, David and Jonathan. In 1776, four years after their father's death, these two brothers recorded a division of this property into two segments, with David receiving the western parcel of 85 acres and Jonathan the eastern parcel of 71 acres. Jonathan sold his parcel to Jirah Wilcox soon thereafter. While there is no record of the transaction, Wilcox is listed as an abutting property owner on the deed whereby David sold his parcel on March 27, 1778, to Jethro Lapham of Glocester. This tract was described in the deed as 'wild and unimproved.'[48] This indicates there was no farming activity or buildings on this property prior to its purchase by Cuff Slocum; nor did he or his sons make improvements on it.

In 1766, Cuff and Ruth Slocum purchased from David Brownell a second property for 650 Spanish milled silver dollars. At the then-prevailing exchange rate of 3¼ silver dollars to the pound, this was roughly equal to £200.[49] Interestingly, David Brownell had purchased the same property one year earlier from Solomon Southwick for 326 Spanish milled silver dollars, indicating he made a considerable profit at the expense of Cuff and Ruth Slocum. This purchase brought the total cost of the two properties purchased by the couple to nearly £300—roughly forty percent of Cuff Slocum's probable earnings over the fifteen years that he worked for Holder Slocum on Cuttyhunk.

This Dartmouth farm was located along the south side of what was referred to in the deeds as "a country road" but what is now known as Old County Road, a well-travelled route from New Bedford to Newport in early times. In 1766, this area was all part of the Town of Dartmouth. When the Town of Westport was divided off from the Town of Dartmouth in 1787, the boundary line was drawn along what is now known as Fisher Road; the eastern boundary of the Cuff Slocum farm was roughly along that road.

A family cemetery that was later located in the northeast corner of the farm and is believed to contain the graves of many descendants of Cuff and Ruth Slocum has been cut off from the original farm by the rerouting of Fisher Road in 1988. That change left the cemetery, now known as the Howard Cemetery, on the southeast corner of the intersection of Fisher Road and Old County Road and within the Town of Dartmouth.

The exact acreage of the farm is unclear. The deed from Brownell to Slocum indicates that it was 120 acres more or less. Later it was depicted in a map of "Cuff Slocum's Farm," drawn up by S. Smith on April 12, 1769, as containing 116 ¾ acres.[50] The date of construction of the original house is also uncertain, but it probably was built between 1736 to 1763, when Enos Gifford owned the property.[51]

At the time that he purchased the farm in 1766, Cuff Slocum also entered into an agreement with David Brownell to provide shingles to re-shingle the east and west ends of the house, further suggesting that the house had been in existence long enough to require re-shingling.[52] It is likely that the land around the house and out-buildings had been at least partially cleared and farmed by the time Cuff Slocum and family moved in. An orchard existed on the farm property.

Enos Gifford had previously granted two approximately 100-acres properties to his two daughters, Rachel Gifford Wilbour and Dorcas Gifford Manchester.

These two properties were to the south of the Cuff Slocum farm, with Rachel's abutting the south boundary of his farm, and Dorcas' abutting the south boundary of Rachel's property.[53]

The Cuff Slocum farm was about 0.8 mile east of the Head of Westport. Developed in the late seventeenth century, this was the first significant settlement area in what became the Town of Westport. Jonathan Soule was the abutter to the west.[54] His brother James would later be appointed as executor of Cuff Slocum's will. Enos Gifford and Phillip Allen were the abutters to the east. Both of them were descendants of early Dartmouth settlers who had bought land from the original proprietors in the 1670s and 1680s.

The original house on Old County Road appears to have been replaced by a newer structure in the latter half of the nineteenth century.[55] Eric Gradoia examined the house and suggested there was evidence that an ell was brought from

*Deed of sale of David Brownell's Dartmouth property to Cuff Slocum.*

To all People to whom these Presents shall come — I, David Brownell, of Dartmouth, in the County of Bristol, in the Province of yᵉ Massachusetts Bay, yeoman — Send Greeting — Know ye, that I yᵉ sᵈ David Brownell, for and in consideration of six hundred and fifty Spanish silver milled dollars to hand before the sealing hereof well and truly paid by Cuff Slocum, of Chilmark, in Dukes County and Province aforesᵈ, the receipt whereof I do hereby acknowledge, and myself therewith fully satisfied, contented and paid, and thereof and of every part and parcel thereof do exonerate, acquit and discharge him, the sᵈ Cuff Slocum, his heirs, exꝑᵗˢ admᵗˢ forever — a certain tract or parcel of land lying in the township of Dartmouth aforesᵈ containing, by estimation, one hundred and twenty acres, be the same more or less, it being bounded as followeth — northerly on the country road — westerly on land belonging to Jonathan Soule — southerly on land Enos Gifford gave to his daughter Rachel Wilbur — easterly partly on said Gifford and partly on Philip Allen's, or according to the Deed I had of Solomon Southwick. To Have and to Hold the sᵈ granted and bargained premises, with all the appurtenances and privileges to the same belonging, or in any wise appertaining to him, yᵉ sᵈ Cuff Slocum, his heirs and assigns forever, to his and their proper use and benefit forever. And I, the sᵈ David

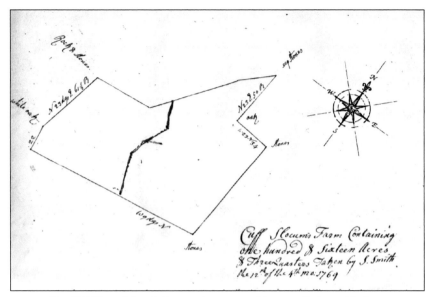

*Plat of Cuff Slocum's farm in Dartmouth. – Courtesy of the New Bedford Free Public Library*

some other property and subsequently added to the east side of main house. The house, at 761 Old County Road, is recorded in the Westport Historic Inventory as probably having belonged at one time to Cuff Slocum.[56] It would be more accurate to say that this property was the site of the original house that Cuff Slocum acquired in 1766 but that the original structure has been replaced.

### Moving to the Farm in Dartmouth

The Cuff Slocum family moved from Cuttyhunk to the new farm in the spring of 1767 in time to plant the crops for the coming growing season. They probably sailed across Buzzards Bay in a shallop, carrying their household belongings with them. These goods undoubtedly included spinning wheels and other instruments for spinning wool and flax into thread for their clothing. When they arrived at their new home, they had a sizeable load of new shingles that Cuff had previously contracted to buy from David Brownell for delivery in March, 1767, so presumably one of their first tasks was to re-shingle the house. This is an indicator that the house was at least 20 years old.

Managing this new farm was very different from the shepherding that Cuff Slocum and his sons had been doing on the islands, but on the other hand, similar to the kind of farm work that Cuff Slocum had probably done for Ebenezer, John and Holder Slocum some years before. They may have hired oxen for plowing their fields and then seeded their crops by hand.[57] Meanwhile, Ruth and her older daughters continued to care for the household chores of fabricating clothing, preparing the food, and caring for the younger daughters. They also had an orchard on the farm, and there is some indication that they may have made cider and sold some of the fruit.[58]

## 1771-72: Cuff Slocum's Will and Passing

In November of 1771, Cuff and Ruth Slocum's oldest son, David, married a woman from Freetown named Hope Page, who was probably a Native American.[59] The following year their second son, Jonathan, married Hepzibah Occouch, whose father was a Wampanoag Indian from Gay Head. Their second daughter, Mary, married Michael Wainer (Micah Quabbin), a Wampanoag from Dartmouth in 1772. Thus, all three of these children married persons of Native American ancestry, replicating the pattern of their parents.

Cuff Slocum died in the spring of 1772, sometime between the marriage of his first son and the next two marriages of his children. There are no records of any obituaries following his death, and we can only speculate that he was probably buried in what is now called the Howard Cemetery at what was once the northeast corner of his farm. But his will, signed and witnessed on August 15, 1771, gives us some significant insights into his state of mind and his relationships with his immediate family and neighbors. Because it is the only document that provides a definitive statement of Cuff Slocum's views on a number of important matters near the end of his life, a transcript is appended to this essay, and important aspects are discussed here.

Cuff Slocum's will begins with an exuberant statement.

> *"I Cuf Slocum formerly a cervant of John Slocum and since by him set free and now a free man in the Township of Dartmouth...in New England, farmer by trade, being in my declining years but through the mercies of almighty God suffered to retain a reasonable understanding, perfect memory & thanks be given unto Almighty God therefore knowing that it is for all men appointed once to die, do for the preventing of future trouble in my family make & ordain this my last will & testament that is to say I give and recommend my soul into the hands of almighty God my master and merciful creator whence I had my first being, and my body I commit to the earth therein to be decently buried at the discretion of my executor herein after named."*

This statement celebrates his freedom and recognizes the person who played the key role in achieving that freedom. It expresses a strong devotion to God and appreciation for such worldly estate it has pleased God to bless him with. It states his profession as a farmer.

The will reveals different treatment of his daughter, Sarah, from that of his other five daughters. Where all other family members—wife, daughters and sons—are always characterized as "well-beloved," Sarah is not. And where the other five daughters are all to receive bequests of £3 each, Sarah is to receive only 5 shillings, or ¼ of a pound. At the time of drawing up his will, Sarah, the eldest daughter, born on Cuttyhunk in 1752, would have been nineteen. We are left to wonder what caused her father to single her out in this way. Might this be what he was referring to by the phrase "for preventing of future trouble in my family"?

An interesting aspect of the will is that the two older boys, David and Jonathan, were bequeathed the Rhode Island property, which was far away and undeveloped, while the two younger sons, John and Paul, along with their mother, were bequeathed the home farm or homestead on which they were living. David had recently married, and Jonathan was to marry soon after his father died. Perhaps Cuff Slocum thought that they were ready to venture forth and take on the challenges of that distant property, whereas John, aged fourteen, and Paul, at twelve, were still living at home when the will was drawn up and therefore best positioned to share with their mother the responsibilities of managing the farm. Still, it is somewhat remarkable that their father saw fit to charge them with such major responsibilities at such young ages. On the other hand, their mother may have provided significant leadership and cohesion for the family.

One topic about which there has been considerable speculation relates to the transition from using the last name of Slocum to that of Cuf or Cuffe. In the will Cuf starts out by naming himself as Cuf Slocum. He then identifies his wife as Ruth Cuf, alias Ruth Slocum, and then proceeds to identify all his children by the last name of Cuf, which transitions into Cufe; he ultimately ends by signing the document as Cufe Slocum. Thus, by 1771, he was using the last name of Cuf or Cufe for all his family members and the name Slocum only for himself. Various authors writing about Paul Cuffe have suggested that it was he who made the decision to adopt the last name of Cuffe, but Cuf's will indicates that by the time Paul was only twelve, his father had already made that transition. Whether the change in last name was a choice made by Cuff Slocum or was requested or recommended by one of the Slocums is still unclear, but it was at least made early on and was a decision in which Paul may not have had much say.

Cuff appointed James Soule, the younger brother of his neighbor Jonathan Soule, as executor of his will. Jonathan and James were the sons of Nathaniel Soule, who owned property on the west bank of the East Branch of the Acoaxet River that later came into the ownership of Cuff Slocum's daughter Mary and her husband, Michael Wainer. James Soule, hatter, was called Cuff's "well beloved friend" in the will. Jonathan Soule was one of three persons appointed to conduct the inventory of Cuff Slocum's personal possessions after he died. All these Soules were descendants of George Soule, who had sailed into Plymouth a hundred-fifty years earlier on the Mayflower. The collaboration of a former slave, albeit some twenty-five years after gaining his freedom, with a well-beloved neighbor and Mayflower descendant is worth noting.

The inventory of Cuff Slocum's personal possessions, other than his two farm properties, was conducted by Jonathan Soule, William Howland, and Benjamin Gifford. They estimated the total value of those possessions at 86 pounds, 6 shillings, and they included two oxen, one cow, eleven sheep, six swine, four geese, five fowls, clothing, bedding, farm implements, lumber and household furniture. Added to the £290 he paid for his two farms at the time of purchase, this would have brought the total value of his estate to £376, a significant economic achievement.

### What Is Remarkable About Cuff Slocum?

In the middle of the eighteenth century, slavery was pervasive in the American colonies. In New England, many families had slaves, including the Quaker Slocums of Dartmouth. Some slaves were treated better than others, but they were still enslaved and subject to the absolute control of their masters. Freed slaves and "Free Blacks" were subject to discrimination and denied many privileges available to white people.

Cuff Slocum as a young boy must have shown signs of intelligence and diligence that caught the attention of the two Slocum families who owned him. And John Slocum, by all indications, bought him with the intent of setting him free, so he perceived the potential in this twenty-five-year-old black man. But once Cuff "earned" his freedom, he more than fulfilled the expectations of his former masters. John Slocum had told him that, if he saved his earnings, he might be able to buy his own home. Cuff indeed saved his money and bought two large farms. Despite being a man of African ancestry and a former slave, Cuff appears to have established friendships and good working relationships with his white neighbors.

Once Cuff became free, he married a Native American woman and together they had ten healthy and remarkable children, whom they encouraged and inspired to lead exemplary lives and help their fellow citizens, especially persons of color.

Cuff and his wife's examples of hard work and religious commitment were reflected in their children. And Paul Cuffe's later efforts to end slavery and improve the lives of Africans in Africa and the western hemisphere undoubtedly had their roots in his father's experiences.

## Transcription of Cufe Slocum's Will[60]

*In the Name of God Amen: I Cuf Slocum formerly a cervant to John Slocum and since by him sett free and Now a free man in the Township of Dartmouth in the County of Bristol in the Province of Massachusetts Bay in New England, farmer by trade, being in my declining years but through the mercies of almighty god suffered to retain a reasonable understanding, perfect memory & thanks be given unto Almighty God therefore knowing that it is for all men appointed once to die, do for the preventing future trouble in my family made & ordain this my last will & testament that is to say principally and first of all I give, I give & recommend my soul into the hands of almighty god my master and merciful creator whence I had my first being & my body I commit to the earth therein to be decently buried and the discretion of my executor herein after named. And touching all such worldly estate wherewith it hath pleased God to bless me in this life, I give devise & dispose of the same in the following manner and form:*

*In primius, I giveth & bequeath unto my well beloved wife Ruth Cuf, Alius Ruth Slocum the use & improvement of one third part of my homestead farm in Dartmouth where I now live together with the right to use and improvement of any one of my rooms which she shall chuse in my now dwelling house for & during the period she shall remain my widow. I give her my said wife that bed & bedding which she generally lodgeth in and upon. All the rest of my household goods I leave in the hands of my said wife for and during the time she shall remain my widow & worn out in my said wife's service, I give unto my five daughters, namely Mary Cuf, Feare Cuf, Lydia Cuf, Ruth Cuf and Freelove Cuf to be equally divided to & amongst them my said five daughters.*

*Item: I give & bequeath unto my daughter Sarah Cuf, the sum of five shillings to be paid unto her within one year after my decease in lawful money by my son Jonathan Cuf.*

*Item: I give & bequeath unto my two well beloved sons, Namely David Cuf and Jonathan Cuf, all that of my farm which I bought of Nicholace Lapham and said farm lyeth in the Township Gochester in the colony of Rhode Island & Providence Plantations in New England reference being had to my deed of conveyance which I hold the same but for a more particular example demonstration of the particular bounds & quantity of said farm all which I give to them my two said sons to be equally devided between them their & each of their heirs and assigns for ever two or three different persons by them chosen to devide the same as aforesaid.*

*Item: I give & and bequeath unto my beloved daughter the sum of three pounds in lawful money meaning my daughter Mary Cufe and to be paid unto her in lawful money of the province above aforesaid by my son David Cufe with in one year after my decease.*

*Item: I give and bequeath unto my well beloved Daughter Lidia Cufe the sum of three pounds to be given unto her by said daughter Lidia Cufe in lawful money of the province afore said by my son David Cufe within two years after my decease.*

*Item: I give and bequeath unto my beloved daughter Ruth Cufe the sum of three pounds to be paid unto her my said daughter Ruth in lawful money of the province aforesaid by my son Jonathan Cufe within two years after my decease.*

*Item: I give and bequeath to my well beloved daughter Freelove Cufe the sum of three pounds in lawful money of the province aforesaid to be paid unto her by my son David Cufe within three years after my decease and in lawful money.*

*Item: My mind and will is that I do will & order that if either of my five daughters Namely Mary Cufe, Feare Cufe, Lidia Cufe, Ruth Cufe & Freelove Cufe should be sick & want house room then I therefore that they or either of them my said five daughters shall have a privilege in my stone bedroom to live which is built in my now dwelling house where I now live for and during the time they or either of them shall live unmarried and no longer.*

*Item: I give and bequeath unto my two well beloved sons Namely John Cufe and Paul Cufe all my homested farm where I now live together with all the houseings & buildings on the farm to be & remain unto them & to each of them during their natural lives, then to their & each of their sons lawfully begotten and each of their bodies forever to their linages & they my two sons are to come into the possession of two thirds of my said homested farm at my decease & and the other third my two said sons are to posess at the time their mother, my wife, shall sease to be my widow. Moreover I give unto my two said sons, viz. John Cufe and Paul Cufe all my husbandry eutencels of what nature or kinde forever together with all my live stock of every sort and kinde that I have. I also give unto them my two said sons, viz. John Cufe and Paul Cufe all my wearing apparel of every sort and kind whatsoever, my husbandry eutencils all my livestock and all my wearing apparel. I give unto my two sons, viz. John Cufe and Paul Cufe to be equeally divided between them my aforesaid sons. I also give unto my son Paul Cufe my fuze gun.*

*Item: my mind and will is that I so will and order my two said sons namely John Cufe and Paul Cufe to provide and keep one cow for their mother, meaning my afore mentioned wife so that she may be reasonably supplied with milk for her own use and comfort during the time she shall remain my widow.*

*Item: I give unto my son John Cufe my bed and bedding to be that bed of mine with a blue and white striped ticken. I give unto my son Paul Cufe my bed and bedding that he commonly sleeps on.*

*Item of this my last will & testament I do nominate, constitute and appoint, make and ordain my well beloved friend Neighbor James Soule the hatter to be the executor of this my last will and testament desiring him as a friend in all love to take a prudent care to see the same duly a & truly fulfilled according to the true intent & meaning hereof and I do hereby utterly disallow, rebucke & disoune all & every other testaments wills legacies and bequests & executors by me in any way before danme willed and bequested. Ratifying and confirming thes & no other to be my last will & testament. In witness whereof I have here unto set my hand & seal this fifteenth day of August in the seventh year of his lord Majesty and in anno Domini, one thousand seven hundred and seventy-one. Signed sealed and...by the said Cufe Slocum with this the afore written to be his last will and testament in the presence of the subscribers:*

Witnesses: Benjamin Earl, Constant Hart, Ephraim Sanford

Cufe Slocum (his own signature)
Date written at the bottom: June 29, 1772

# Ruth Cuffe's Testimonial
## About Her Grandfather's Freedom
## And Some Interesting Related Stories

*I*N 1851, JAMES B. Congdon, an early researcher into the life of Paul Cuffe, apparently invited Ruth Cuffe to write down her memories about how her grandfather, Cuff Slocum, gained his freedom. That document, preserved in the New Bedford Free Public Library's collection of papers relating to Paul Cuffe, provides fascinating insights into the Cuff Slocum story and to the interconnections among families descended from Cuff Slocum—the Cuffes and the Wainers—and also among the families that freed him and interacted with him on his way to success as a free man—the Slocums and the Hulls.

Ruth Cuffe's testimonial, written in 1851, recounts a story that she was told fifty-three years before, in 1798, when she was only seven years old…and the story describes events that probably occurred fifty-three years before that, going back all the way to 1745. Given such long periods between the actual events in 1745 and the transcription of the story in 1851, it is not unreasonable to expect some factual errors, but the basic story does appear to hold together if some of the key actors are re-identified.

We start off with a transcription of the full document as written by Ruth Cuffe and follow that with comments on the individuals identified in it and some hypotheses as to possible corrections regarding the people in the story.

*As nigh as I can remember it was fifty-three years ago that I was to work at my brother-in-law Gardner Wainer's in Westport on the eastern side of the River and my sister wanted me to go to the store at Russeles mill in Dartmouth and buy her some things out of the store. She told me to go to Captain Hull's store and do my trading for she had all their trading done at his store and I went for her, and when I got their, their was several men in the store and Mr. Hull told me to take a seat and sit down and wait a little while till he had waited upon them men and then he would waite upon me and as soon as they was gone out of the store he asked me what my name was. I told him that my name was Ruth Cuffe. He asked me what my father's name was. I told him that my father's name was David Cuffe.*

*Then Mr. Hull told me that my grandfather Cuffe was a slave man to his father. He told me that his father bought my grandfather Cuffe so that he should have his freedom, and his father wrote down the month and day that he purchased him and how many dollars he gave for him, and when grandfather Cuffe had worked long enough to pay for himself then his master freed him. His master paid him good wages and when he had worked long enough to pay for himself, his master gave him his freedom. The day before, he went to a Squire's house and had a paper rote to give Cuffe his freedom and the next morning the Squire brought the paper* to his house and carried the paper with him and he got there just as they were sitting down to breakfast and they all sat down and Cuffe with them and after they had some breakfast the Squire told Cuffe to take his seat as he wanted to talk with him. The Squire then asked him did he want to be a free man and be his own man. He said that he wanted to be free but he had no money to buy himself and he wanted his master not to sell him to no one and when he made his will to give his children his property to fix it so that his children never should sell him for he was afraid that he would be sold away to the west and put on the plantation. His master told him that never should be. The squire told Cuffe that he would be a free man in a few minutes. He then took the paper out of his pocket and showed it to Cuffe. The squire told Mr. Hull to write his name on the paper and he did. And then he told Hull's wife to write her name on the same paper and she did. Then the squire gave the paper over again to Cuffe and told him he then was a free man – his own man and he must go from there that same day. Then Cuffe cried and covered himself with tears. He said that he did not know what to do and where to go he knew not. He had no home and no money for food that they had ought to let him know of it 2 or 3 weeks ago. Then it would not be so hard to him for then it was a rainy day and where to go he knew not. The squire told him that he must certainly go from there that day for that would show that he was his own free man and gone from there. The squire told him he would hire him and give him good wages. He hired him right away, and his master Hull though would hire him next month and give him good wages. The squire then gave Cuffe his paper that he wrote and told him to put into his chest in his protection carrying it with him at his house and keep it safe. Then his master that had been, gave Cuffe good advice while the squire was there. He told him to live a steady life and to take good care of his money that he was going to work for and save it so as to get him a home some-time or other. So Cuffe took 2 suits of his everyday clothes and went away from there that same day.

This Captain Hull told me at the time I was in his store and he said about the time my grandfather Cuffe had his freedom, Ruth Moses came up from Harawig, and after a while my grandfather married her. She came into Dartmouth and worked their till she married and Captain Hull told me that the Slocomes would not have my grandfather Cuffe's children to go by the name of Slocumbes so they called them by their father's name Cuffe. I was about seven years old when we had to go by the name of Cuffe. I remember it well.

**Family relations of persons mentioned in the story: Cuffes and Wainers**

Ruth Cuffe states that she was the daughter of David Cuffe. David was the first son of Cuff and Ruth (Moses) Slocum, born in Dartmouth in 1748. David married Hope Page of Freetown in 1771. His younger sister, Mary (b. 1753), married Michael Wainer (b. 1748) in 1772. David and Hope (Page) Cuffe had six children, the third being Rhoda and the fifth being Ruth. Rhoda married Gardner Wainer, the second son of Michael and Mary (Cuffe) Wainer and therefore Mary's first cousin. Ruth Cuffe never married but lived in Indian Town in the North Westport and Troy (Fall River) border area and was reportedly a "Doctress" in later life.

Ebenezer Slocum (b. 1705) was born in Dartmouth and was the first owner of Cuff Slocum, having purchased him in Newport, Rhode Island around 1728. He married Bathsheba Hull in Newport, where the bride lived, in 1728. Bathsheba Hull was the daughter of Tristram Hull and Elizabeth Dyer. A genealogy chart shows the ancestors of Rebecca and Bathsheba Hull and linkages between the Hull and Slocum families in the eighteenth century.

Bathsheba was the great-granddaughter of Tristram Hull (b. 1624), an early settler of Barnstable, Massachusetts. Her line ran from Tristram through Joseph (b. 1651) to Tristram (b. 1677). Bathsheba was also the granddaughter of Mary Dyer, who was hanged on Boston Common in 1660 for preaching Quaker heresy.

Another descendant of Tristram Hull was Hannah Hull (b. 1697), whose lineage ran from Tristram through John Hull (b. 1654). She married Holder Slocum (b. 1697) of Dartmouth in 1721. Holder Slocum was a cousin of Ebenezer Slocum and played an important role in the lives of Cuff and Ruth Slocum.

### Who actually told the story about Cuff Slocum?

Ebenezer Slocum sold Cuff Slocum to his nephew, John Slocum (b. 1717), son of his brother, Eliezer (b. 1694). This transaction is recorded in a deed of sale dated February 16, 1742, which describes Cuff Slocum as a negro man of about twenty-five years of age. The price paid for Cuff Slocum was £150. (See p. 39.)

The release of Cuff Slocum from slavery and making him a free man, as described in Ruth Cuffe's testimonial, took place probably about three years after John Slocum purchased him in 1742. According to Ruth's story, the owner of the store in which she was told the story was a Captain Hull, and he said that it was his father who freed Cuff Slocum many years before.

While there definitely was a store owned by a Captain Hull in the Russells Mills section of Dartmouth at that time (around 1800), there is clear evidence that it was not his father who freed Cuff Slocum. The deed of sale clearly establishes that it was John Slocum who purchased Cuff in 1742, and the first sentence of Cuff Slocum's will from 1772 states that

> I Cuf Slocum formerly a cervant of John Slocum and thence by him sett free and now a free man,.

Thus, the questions are: Who could rightly claim that his father had been the one to set Cuff Slocum free? And who might have been the person telling the story to Ruth Slocum about the freeing of her grandfather? Is it possible that Ruth misunderstood when Captain Hull said it was his father rather than someone else's father?

There are two people who were, according to the story, involved in the process of freeing Cuff—the owner and the squire. The owner was definitely John Slocum, but who was the squire? It is our belief that the squire was Holder Slocum, a prominent resident of Dartmouth and a first cousin once removed of John Slocum. Holder Slocum was the person who subsequently employed Cuff Slocum to look after his livestock during the summer grazing season on the three western Elizabeth Islands he owned. He may well have hired Cuff Slocum immediately after the latter gained his freedom, as Ruth Cuffe's story indicates was the stated intention of the squire.

Given that John Slocum and probably Holder Slocum were the two persons who were involved in the act of giving Cuff Slocum his freedom, it seems likely that the storyteller in Captain Hull's store was either a son of John Slocum or a son of Holder Slocum. The fact that Holder Slocum Jr. was an executor of Captain Hull's estate along with his widow, Abigail, after his death in 1807 would seem to tip the scale toward Holder Slocum Jr. Or, perhaps, Captain Hull may have been repeating a story told to him by Holder Slocum Jr and Ruth Cuffe just misunderstood him.

## Lineages of Holder and John Slocum

Holder Slocum (b. 1697) and Ebenezer Slocum (b. 1705) were first cousins, both descendants of a common grandfather, Giles Slocum (c1620-1682). Their fathers were Peleg (b. 1654) and Eliezer (b. 1664) respectively. John Slocum (b. 1717) was a great-grandson of Giles Slocum, a grandson of Eliezer and a son of Eliezer Jr. (b. 1694).

Holder Slocum's son, Christopher Slocum (b. 1738), inherited the three western Elizabeth Islands—Nashawena, Pasque, and Cuttyhunk—from his father after he died in 1758. He continued the practice of grazing sheep on those islands, as suggested by the fact that, before she died in 1773, he billed his mother (Rebecca Almy Slocum) £60 for grazing her 285 sheep for three years; this obligation was listed in her inventory after her death.

John Slocum (b.1717) married Deborah Almy in Dartmouth in 1738, and they had two sons, John Jr. and William, who subsequently lived on Pasque and Nashawena. John Slocum Jr. (b. 1746 in Dartmouth) married Rhobea Briggs on October 9, 1767, and they are reported in the Slocum genealogy to have lived on Pasque Island for several years before moving to Nashawena, where he died in 1818. It is not clear whether they moved to Pasque immediately after their marriage, but it may be noted that their marriage occurred in the same year that Cuff Slocum moved his family from Cuttyhunk to their new farm in Dartmouth. It is conceivable that John Slocum Jr. took over responsibility for overseeing sheep-grazing activities on his uncle Holder Slocum Jr.'s three islands. William Slocum (b. 1769) married Mary Cheney in 1792. He was a master-mariner for many years, and later in life, a farmer with residence on Nashawena Island.

We have not been able to establish the relationship between the Captain Hull who owned the store in Russells Mills in 1800 and the previous Hulls, Rebecca and Bathsheba, who were descended from Tristram Hull (1624) and married Holder and Ebenezer Slocum respectively. But we will keep searching.

There are several interesting stories in the Slocum genealogy and in the book about the Elizabeth Islands by Alice Forbes Howland that are worth retelling because they are from sources that are not easily available. The first is from the sketch of Holder Slocum Sr. in the Slocum genealogy (pp. 67-8).

## Holder Slocum Sr. provides a shallop for a Quaker minister to sail to Nantucket.

Thomas Chalkley, a distinguished minister in the Society of Friends, wrote that Holder Slocum was prominent among Friends as early as the time of his marriage to Captain Hull's daughter. Thomas Chalkley visited Dartmouth in the

# Descendant Chart of Giles and Joan Slocum

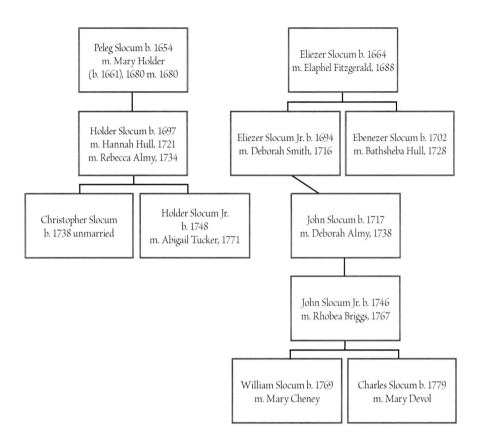

Peleg Slocum b. 1654
m. Mary Holder
(b. 1661), 1680 m. 1680

Eliezer Slocum b. 1664
m. Elaphel Fitzgerald, 1688

Holder Slocum b. 1697
m. Hannah Hull, 1721
m. Rebecca Almy, 1734

Eliezer Slocum Jr. b. 1694
m. Deborah Smith, 1716

Ebenezer Slocum b. 1702
m. Bathsheba Hull, 1728

Christopher Slocum
b. 1738 unmarried

Holder Slocum Jr.
b. 1748
m. Abigail Tucker, 1771

John Slocum b. 1717
m. Deborah Almy, 1738

John Slocum Jr. b. 1746
m. Rhobea Briggs, 1767

William Slocum b. 1769
m. Mary Cheney

Charles Slocum b. 1779
m. Mary Devol

## Descendant Chart from Cuff Slocum and Ruth Moses

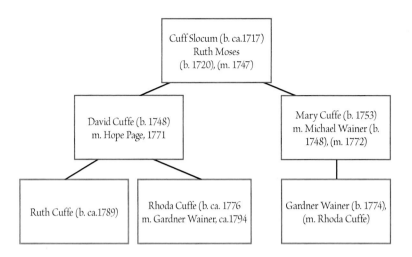

Cuff Slocum (b. ca.1717)
Ruth Moses
(b. 1720), (m. 1747)

David Cuffe (b. 1748)
m. Hope Page, 1771

Mary Cuffe (b. 1753)
m. Michael Wainer (b. 1748), (m. 1772)

Ruth Cuffe (b. ca.1789)

Rhoda Cuffe (b. ca. 1776
m. Gardner Wainer, ca.1794

Gardner Wainer (b. 1774), (m. Rhoda Cuffe)

## Hull Descendants married to Slocums

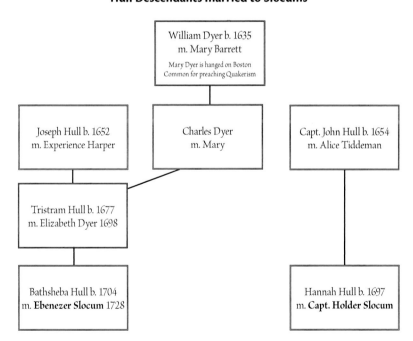

William Dyer b. 1635
m. Mary Barrett
Mary Dyer is hanged on Boston
Common for preaching Quakerism

Joseph Hull b. 1652
m. Experience Harper

Charles Dyer
m. Mary

Capt. John Hull b. 1654
m. Alice Tiddeman

Tristram Hull b. 1677
m. Elizabeth Dyer 1698

Bathsheba Hull b. 1704
m. **Ebenezer Slocum** 1728

Hannah Hull b. 1697
m. **Capt. Holder Slocum**

year 1737 and was entertained at the house of Captain Slocum. His *Journal,* on that occasion, contains the following entry:

> Holder Slocum lent us his shallop to go over to Nantucket; but the wind not favoring, we had a satisfactory meeting at a large farm of his on an island bearing his own name, and after the meeting set sail for Nantucket; had several large meetings there, and I rejoiced to see the growth and increase of Friends on the island, where God hath greatly multiplied his people and made them honorable.'

Slocum's Island, referred to above, was probably Nashawena Island, next to Cuttyhunk in Buzzards Bay. Holder's first wife, Hannah, died at her father's house in Jamestown, Rhode Island, on August 28, 1725 and was buried there in Friends' ground. His second marriage, to Rebecca Almy of Tiverton, Rhode Island, took place on January 4, 1733 or 1734.

This sketch attests to several interesting facts:

- Shallops were popular small sailing and rowing craft used for traveling along the New England coast and to the nearby islands.
- Holder Slocum had a "large farm" on one of the Elizabeth Islands, probably either Nashawena or Pasque, in 1737. It is not clear what kind of farm it was. While some evidence points to a sheep station for warm weather grazing, it could have been used for something else. Nor is it clear how many people were living on the island, if they lived there year-round, or whether there were substantial dwellings on the property; the sketch does suggest, however, that there were some people residing there for at least part of the year at that time.

### More insights on the activities of the Slocums on the Elizabeth Islands

The insights from the Slocum genealogy are further reinforced by excerpts from the book by Alice Forbes Howland: *Three Islands: Pasque, Nashawena and Penikese* (pp 57-60).

> Although Peleg Slocum seems to have owned Nashawena from 1693 until it was acquired by his son Holder in 1742, it would not appear that he ever lived on the island and it is pretty clear that he lived on his big farm at Barney's Joy across the Bay. He evidently owned at least one boat which he sailed himself, occasionally to Nantucket to hold or attend Quaker meetings.

> Nashawena and Cuttyhunk afforded good summer grazing in those days, and cattle were taken over from the mainland in boats each spring and brought back in the autumn. The old stone pound where the cattle were rounded up for these trips is still standing (1964) near the mouth of Slocum's River, and it may be supposed that Peleg sent his own cattle over to the island, and perhaps those of some of his neighbors as well, for which grazing privileges they would have paid him a fee.

> Peleg died in 1733 at the age of 79. In 1743 Peleg's son Holder, then 46 years old, came into possession of part of the east end of Nashawena from 'fellmonger' (a dealer in sheepskins or other hides) Thomas Bailey and others. Eight years later in 1751, Holder acquired all of the land on Nashawena, Cuttyhunk and Penikese that Peleg had owned... We know little of Holder's activities or if he ever lived on the island, but inasmuch as his son, Holder Jr. is listed as 'of Dartmouth' in a Court Record in 1794

*against John Slocum of Chilmark (remember that Nashawena was part of the town of Chilmark in those days), it would seem that Holder Jr. owned the island but lived on the mainland while John lived either on Nashawena or Pasque.*

*Now comes a gap in our story as there appears to be nothing to tell us what happened on Nashawena or who was living there from 1745 to the time of the Revolution. As early as 1775 the British Sloop of War Faulkland made a surprise visit to the Elizabeth Islands and seized livestock from Naushon and Pasque, and it is more than likely that they took cattle, sheep and hogs from Nashawena as well; so those years when British warships were continually in the waters of the Bay and Sound must have been a time of fear and deprivation for the people living on the islands.*

In an earlier part of her story, Howland reports that life on Pasque and Nashawena was not always so dismal or uninteresting. In her chapters on Pasque, she tells the following story (pp. 6-7):

*Pasque was the scene of a small but relatively important intrigue in 1779 when a group of British officers from a fleet lying in Tarpaulin Cove 'spent the evening of April 2nd in a frolic at the house of John Slocum on Pesque (sic) Island" Now, Slocum was a Quaker and well-known for his Tory sympathies, but after hearing his 'guests' discussing plans to attack and burn Falmoth the following day, loyalty to his neighbors overcame his Tory leanings, and he sent a messenger secretly down the island and across to the mainland to warn the people there of their danger. The British met a well-organized force of militia, which had been hastily summoned from Barnstable and Sandwich, and were successfully repulsed; and they must have wondered how their plans – laid so carefully two islands and ten miles away – could have been anticipated.*

Christopher, the oldest son of Holder and Rebecca Slocum, had inherited Cuttyhunk from his father and later passed it and other properties in the Elizabeth Islands along to his two brothers, Peleg and Holder Slocum Jr. The inventory of his mother's estate shows that Christopher had billed his mother, Rebecca Slocum, £60 for grazing her 285 sheep on Cuttyhunk for three years, suggesting that the annual charge for grazing this number of sheep was £20. Unfortunately, we have no way of estimating how many sheep might have been grazing on the western Elizabeth Islands that Christopher Slocum and his brothers owned at that time.

Also included in the inventory of Rebecca Slocum's estate was a "ferryboat lying at Christopher Slocum's wharf together with her anchor, rigging, sails and appurtenances" valued at £43, 6 shillings and 8 pence. This would be a reasonable description of a shallop.

### What can we learn from these stories?

- Peleg Slocum owned at least Nashawena from 1693 until his death in 1743 when it passed to his oldest son, Holder Slocum. But Holder appears, according to Rev. Chalkley's story, to have been in charge of activities there in 1733 which included some kind of a farm.

- Holder Slocum inherited at least parts of Nashawena from his father and by 1751 owned three islands—Nashawena, Cuttyhunk and Penikese. Alice Howland says that there is no record of what happened on these islands between 1751 and 1775, when the British Navy raided them and took away livestock.

- From our previous research, we can fill this gap that links to Ruth Cuffe's testimonial. Cuff Slocum and Ruth Moses were married in Dartmouth in 1748 and had their first two children, David and Jonathan, in Dartmouth in 1748 and 1749. Their third child, Sarah, was born in 1752 on Cuttyhunk. Cuff and Ruth Slocum had their next seven children on Cuttyhunk between1753 to 1766. We have concluded that Cuff was working for Holder Slocum looking after the livestock, mainly sheep, that were brought to at least Cuttyhunk and Nashawena during those years. The family moved to Dartmouth in the spring of 1767 to a 116-acre farm they had purchased from David Brownell. We also know from the Slocum genealogical story that John Slocum (b. 1746) married Rhobea Briggs in 1767 and that they moved to Pasque sometime thereafter. Whether they took over management of the livestock grazing activities on the western Elizabeth Islands from Cuff Slocum we don't know, but we do have the evidence, from Christopher Slocum's claim on his mother's estate in 1773 for three years of grazing 285 of her sheep on Cuttyhunk, that such livestock (probably mainly sheep) grazing continued up until that time. And then the British raid on several Elizabeth Islands in 1775 to take livestock confirms the continuing practice.

- John and Rhobea Slocum were still living on Pasque in 1779 when they entertained the British naval officers in their home and then alerted the people of Falmouth to the impending attack the next day.

- There is no record of when John Slocum and his family moved to Nashawena. It may have been sometime during the Revolutionary War. But it is clear that this Slocum family, and possibly others, were living on the western Elizabeth Islands during the war, and John is said to have been a loyalist.

- It is worth noting that during these war years, Paul Cuffe, the son of Cuff Slocum, was sailing through these western Elizabeth Islands, probably in a shallop borrowed from one of the Dartmouth-based Slocums, to deliver supplies to the Quaker and partly loyalist inhabitants of Nantucket. It would be surprising if he did not have some interactions with family members of John Slocum Sr., who had purchased and then freed his father, during his travels back and forth through those islands.

- The 1794 court record of a lawsuit brought by Holder Slocum Jr. of Dartmouth (b. 1748) against his cousin John Slocum (probably John Slocum Jr. of Chilmark [b. 1746]) suggests that these cousins were not always able to settle their affairs amicably and that John Slocum was probably at that time still engaged in activities on the island of Nashawena, then owned by his cousin, Holder Jr.

# Exploring Cuff Slocum's Book:
## The Exercise Book and Book of Accounts

*O*NE OF THE important sources of insight into the life of Cuff Slocum and his family is the document preserved at the New Bedford Free Public Library entitled "Exercise Book and Book of Accounts of Cuffe Slocum." For many years, this document was available to the public only on microfilm at the New Bedford Free Public Library, and it was very tedious to scroll through and analyze. But it was recently copied digitally and is now available on a number of websites.[61] This has made it much easier to study the document in detail and compare the handwriting on different pages to gain a better comprehension of the contents.

An initial realization is that the entries were written not just by Cuff Slocum; clearly there are entries by others. The challenge, then, is to try to figure out who the other writers might have been and why their entries may have found their way into this particular notebook. Probably an even greater and more important challenge is to tease out the various bits of information contained in this document and put them into some kind of context of Cuff Slocum's life and those of his family's..

In the following discussion, we will look at the different styles of writing, then at the content of some of the excerpts, and finally mesh some of the messages with what we already know of Cuff Slocum's life. This first entry is an example of Cuff Slocum's writing and his typical pattern of practicing the writing of the alphabet.

*– Courtesy of the New Bedford Free Public Library*

### Different writing styles

Copied below is the first page of Cuff Slocum's Exercise Book. It provides a good example of his writing both in terms of writing style and content. The style is rough and crude, but distinctly of his style as it shows up later in the book. In some cases, the entries are written in printed letters, and in others it is cursive. The content is typical in that it starts at the top with practice writing of the alphabet.

This is followed by numerous random entries, some of which appear to be practice exercises in writing some words. There are several references to pounds and shillings, which was the currency of his time, and also a reference to the town of Chilmark. Cuttyhunk at that time was a part of the town of Chilmark, so he was practicing writing the name of the town in which he lived.

One discernable phrase is: "I promise to pay," followed by undecipherable words. Below that is a practice line: "year month week day night."

On the opposite page, the excerpt is from later in the book. It contains at the top Cuff Slocum's usual practicing of the alphabet in mostly cursive lower-case letters, and in the next row, in capital letters.

The writing in the lower part of the page is distinctly different. It presents, in well-formed cursive writing, a listing of the birth dates of all ten children of Cuff

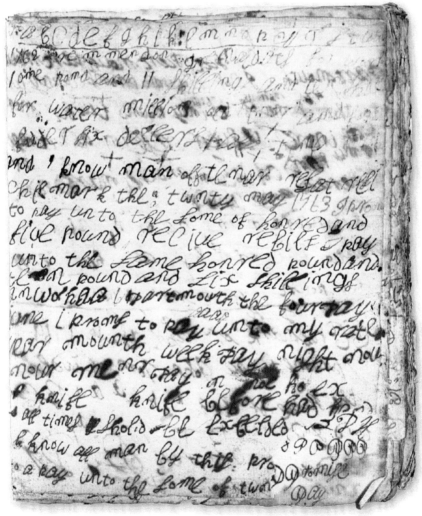

*– Courtesy of the New Bedford Free Public Library*

and Ruth Slocum. It gives the location of Dartmouth before the first-born son, David, but makes no further mention of the location of the other births. All of the entries are very personal—"my son" or "my daughter," for example—as though the writer was their mother, Ruth Moses Slocum. Initially, we thought that this might be an indication that she had written these entries, but the fact that she signed with her mark on a document releasing her rights of dower after her husband's death in 1772 suggests either that she did not know how to write or chose in that instance not to. We cannot know.

At the end of this page is the mathematical calculation of the number of years between the first and last births of Cuff and Ruth's children, i.e. 18 years, then spelled out more precisely as "17 years, 3 months and 19 days."

## Building a house for Rebecca Slocum

In the next excerpts, we have two examples relating the same story. The first appears to be written by Cuff Slocum, whereas the second is by someone else with more skilled handwriting.

The two entries record that: "in 1764 Master Rebeker Slocum had a debt to Cuff for work on a house at Cutthunker." Next comes this entry: When the house was raised, I was work three days for 9 shillings. Second time kfend come I work 5 days 15 shillings. When mason come I work 12 ½ day one pound 17 shilling 6 pence and my boy work 12 ½ days one pound 17sh 6 pence lawful money." The final entry in the lower document, written in October of 1770, indicates a "Capen Potter debt to one gallon melon 13 4, two quart rum 9 s(hillings.)"

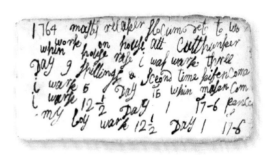

These entries provide a number of interesting insights:

- The house for Rebecca Slocum, widow of Holder Slocum, was built in 1764 on Cuttyhunk Island.

- Cuff Slocum helped to build the house but was not the primary builder.

*– Courtesy of the New Bedford Free Public Library*

- The principal builders probably came over to Cuttyhunk by boat from Dartmouth and brought the various building materials with them.

- Cuff and one of his sons, probably David, the eldest, helped a mason for 12 ½ days each.

- The rate of pay for both Cuff and his son was 3 shillings per day.

- Their total earnings for the work on the house was 4 pounds, 18 shillings, 12 pence, or nearly 5 pounds for 33 days of work.

- The price for two quarts of rum was 9 shillings, the equivalent of 3 days of work.

## Who was Mary Prince?

On the next page, the Exercise Book shows that Cuff had a number of dealings with a woman named Mary Prince. She may have been a neighbor on Cuttyhunk or one of the nearby islands. His first transaction is for "fore shillings and six penc old (tenor)." On the next three lines: half boshil (bushel) flix (flax) seed done by 1764 25 day Mary Prince half boshil corn and five pounds fat for half pound fat corn half boshil, Mary Prince; and "for three pound wool and a half boshil corn…." There are several other entries for Mary Prince on the page.

There is a marriage record of a Mary Prince, "Mustee," d. Mary (widow), and Ceser Slocum, "Negro man belonging to Christopher Slocum," intentions, Apr. 26, 1775. Given the year of this event, it is likely that it was the mother of this Mary Prince, also named Mary Prince, who would have been dealing with Cuff Slocum. The probability of this is increased by the fact that the daughter was marrying a slave belonging to Christopher Slocum, the son of Holder and Rebecca Slocum and the owner of Cuttyhunk at the time of their intentions.

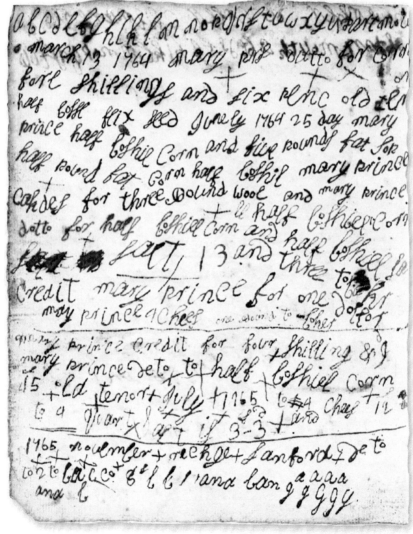

## Writing by John Cuffe

The page from the Cuff Slocum Exercise Book shown below appears to be written by John Cuffe in 1776, four years after his father's death. It is difficult to decipher and may have been a practice writing of a message that was later transcribed on another document. But it gives an indication of John's writing style and his signature. A number of his letters are also available in the Paul Cuffe Papers.

## Charges for room and board

The entry at the top of the next page, while dated "Chilmark 1764," probably applies to Cuttyhunk Island, which belonged to Chilmark at the time. It indicates

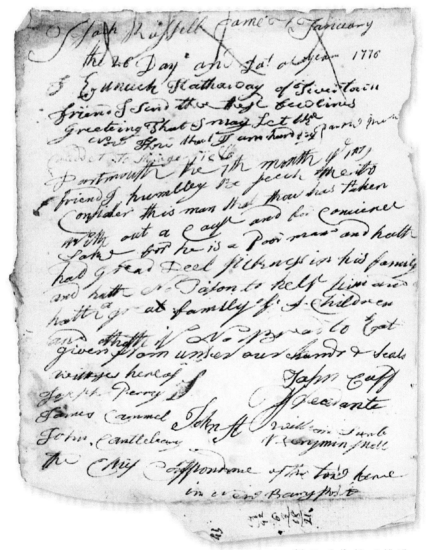

*– Courtesy of the New Bedford Free Public Library*

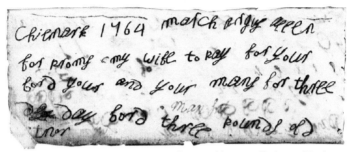

that someone had promised to pay Cuff Slocum's wife "for your board and your mans for three days the amount of three pounds old tenor." Given the year of this transaction, it raises the question as to whether these boarders might have been put up in Rebecca Slocum's new cottage on Cuttyhunk and that Ruth Slocum prepared their meals. It seems very unlikely that they could have stayed in Cuff Slocum's house with their nine children at that time. There is no indication as to who the boarder was, but he might well have been a friend of the Slocums staying in their house with their blessing.

### An uncertain quotation

There are two excerpts from Cuff Slocum's Exercise Book that have been quoted in writings about Paul Cuffe, which indicate the true nature and purpose of Cuff. The first, in Cuff's own writing, says (as can best be determined): "Do

good to all and and mind." Then written directly under that in more stylized script this is repeated: "Do good to all and mind not to." Clearly, neither statement has been completed, so one can only guess what the remainder might have been.

Later in the exercise book there is an entry that may or may not be by the same writer, which says: "Do good all. Do good to all. Do good at all time, larn read. Cuffe Slocum mister." It is this latter version that has been quoted and attributed to Cuff Slocum. But it is clearly not his handwriting. Whether it reflects something that he said to the writer or it was the writer's interpretation and expansion of the phrase cited above is unclear, but the fact that it reflects Cuff Slocum's philosophy is unquestioned.

### An enigma

The entry at right is an enigma.
It refers to a person by the name of
Domingo dice Ro?ay. This is prefaced
by the phrase "Celnd opened Book of."
We do not know when this entry was

made or by whom. But the name is of interest because Cuff and Ruth's daughter
Sarah married a Mingo Dice in 1782. Sarah was treated differently than her other
five sisters in her father's will, suggesting that she might have been in disfavor, or
already provided for by him, or something else. This entry might be an indicator
that Sarah was already involved in some way with Domingo Dice while her father
was still alive. Regardless, it is a fact that this name appears in the Cuff Slocum
Exercise Book at some point in time. It is not clear if he had a last name or if the
word at the end of his name refers to something else. As stated above: an enigma.

### What have we learned from the Exercise Book?

Cuff Slocum's Exercise Book and Book of Accounts contains forty-seven pages.
Many of them contain information about transactions in commodities or services
that Cuff Slocum was engaged in. We have presented only a limited selection here,
but it gives a sense of the broader content and provides information on specific
activities or persons that are of special interest.

### Here is a summary of the most important findings:

- The book contains the writings of a number of people, including Cuff Slocum
  and probably some members of his family.
- It is not possible to identify the writer with the good cursive script who listed
  the birth dates of the children and repeated some of the earlier notes that Cuff
  had written.
- The entries are spread over a number of years, with the earliest being 1764 and
  the last in 1780.
- The entries confirm Cuff and his son's role in building the house for Rebecca
  Slocum.
- They also show that he sold various commodities to a person named Mary
  Prince, who probably lived nearby on Cuttyhunk or a neighboring island.
- Cuff's wife, Ruth, was paid for providing board and room for some visitors
  who stayed overnight on Cuttyhunk.
- The birth dates of all the children of Cuff and Ruth Slocum are confirmed, but
  the location of their births is not.
- The name of Domingo Dice, who later married daughter Sarah, appears in the
  book, but there is no record of when or why it was written.
- The statement of Cuff Slocum's philosophy that has been quoted in various
  places appears to be an elaboration of his original writing but is not inconsis-
  tent with his apparent thought and behavior.

# New Revelations from Old Deeds:
## The Properties of Paul Cuffe and Michael Wainer

OVER THE LAST few decades, there has been growing interest in and research on the lives of Paul Cuffe; his father, Cuff Slocum; and his brother-in-law, Michael Wainer. Various authors have speculated on where they lived and what properties they owned. As new sources have become available or more accessible, we have found that the properties attributed to the three of them have been incorrect in many cases. The most significant discovery is that the property at 1504 Drift Road in Westport, recorded as "Paul Cuffe's Farm" on both the National Register of Historic Places and the Massachusetts Historical Commission's Inventory of Historic Assets of the Commonwealth was in fact not his farm/homestead. A portion of this paper is devoted to identifying his correct homestead.

The property holdings of Cuff Slocum have already been discussed in Chapter Five and will not be described here as they were in previous versions of this paper.[62]

In the process of researching these matters, we spent considerable time in the Bristol County Registry of Deeds offices in Taunton and New Bedford as well as the Probate Records department in Taunton. We also collected much additional information that we felt shed light on not only the properties owned by Paul Cuffe, Cuff Slocum and Michael Wainer, but also on the families and activities of the prior and contemporary residents and property owners of the South Coast region of Massachusetts.

Herein we share that information along with our sources so that others who are interested can trace those records and verify or question our findings. Three other families, the Sowles (Soules), the Eddys, and the Allens, were particularly important to our research and we have added additional information about them in appendices.

### Paul Cuffe's Properties

There has been much conjecture and debate about where Paul Cuffe lived, where he had his docks and boatyards, and where his "homestead," his windmill, salt works, "machine lot," "Allen lot" and "meeting house" properties were located. Paul Cuffe owned many properties in Westport and Dartmouth during his lifetime, some of which were included in his will or in the later inventory of his estate, but the will and inventory do not provide information about their location. We have attempted to pin down the locations and uses of those properties. We note that his ownership of some of the properties was the result of mortgage-based loans he made to several widows of friends or relatives or business activities in which he was engaged.

## An Overview

In the spring of 1767, as described previously, Paul Cuffe moved with his family to the farm that his father had recently purchased in Dartmouth (now Westport). That farm was most likely his home base for at least the next fifteen years.

He is recorded as living in an Indian Style house in 1783, the year he married Alice Abel Pequit. There is no record of how long he and Alice lived in that house, but a Caleb Briggs was living in that house in 1788, so by then they had moved elsewhere. Paul had inherited the western half of his father's farm, which included the house and barns. His mother had the right of occupancy on the property until she died in 1787, but Paul, Alice, and their growing family may well have resided in that farm home while his mother was still alive.

In 1789, two years after his mother's death, Paul purchased a small property from Isaac Soule on the west bank of the East Branch of the Acoaxet River, where he established his shipyard. He probably moved to a residence at or near that property by 1790, when he is recorded in the national census along with other neighboring families in that area. He had definitely built a substantial house there by 1798, when his residence is recorded as being valued at $620 in a national tax assessment. He increased the size of this riverfront holding in 1800 by about one-half through a purchase from Lemuel Soule. He then increased this holding by four acres in 1813 by a purchase from David Soule and this remained his homestead until he died in 1817. All of these acquisitions and holdings are described in greater detail below.

## Paul and Alice (Pequit) Cuffe's Indian-Style House

On February 25, 1783 Paul Cuffe and Alice Abel Pequit were officially married in Dartmouth, Massachusetts, and on September 23rd of that year, they were recorded as living in an Indian-style house in a deed transferring a 600-acre property from Timothy Russell to William Snell.

This deed has very complicated lines and bounds, but it refers back to a 1772 survey of the property recorded in "The field notes" of Benjamin Crane, Benjamin Hamilton, and Samuel Smith. The field notes indicate that the survey of Timothy Russell's farm included the adjoining lots of John Russell.

The beginning of the statement of lines and bounds in the Russell to Snell deed states: "beginning at an old maple tree in the brook or ditch for a corner bound in Destruction Swamp." This deed later has the following provision:

> The above bounds and lines include nine acres and a half over and above ye above said six hundred acres which...is not here conveyed. Three acres thereof I formerly sold to a Mullato man called Clarence Gray as reference being had to ye deed of conveyance thereof... Six acres thereof I have sold to James Fisher whereon said Fisher's dwelling house stands and is bounded off by deed as may appear. The other half-acre is that whereon an Indian Style house stands that Paul Cuff now lives in."

It is not possible to determine exactly where this Indian-style house was located, but it was probably near Destruction Swamp and Brook, along what is now known as Fisher Road, which may have some connection to James Fisher's

*The Indian-style house where newlyweds Paul and Alice Cuffe lived*
*may have looked like this wetu. – Watercolor by Raymond C. Shaw*

dwelling house. It is also not clear whether Paul Cuffe owned this property or was just occupying a house on the property. The deed does not mention Paul Cuffe's ownership, as it does for the Gray and Fisher properties.

There is no record of how long Paul and Alice Cuffe lived in this house, but the Notebooks of Henry Worth record that in 1788 this "Indian House" was occupied by Caleb Briggs. In the 1790 census, Caleb Briggs was a neighbor to Henry Gidley, Elijah Macomber, Samuel Gidley, John Ricketson, James Fisher, Eliphalet Packard, Noah Packard, and Stephen Russell, all familiar names along Fisher Road north of Destruction Brook toward Gidley Town.

### Paul Cuffe's Wharf and Shipyard

Paul Cuffe purchased his first property on the west bank of the East Branch of the Acoaxet River on March 19, 1789, from Isaac Sowle for four pounds, 18 shillings and 5 pence.

The property, carved out of the southeast corner of Isaac Sowle's homestead, contained 35 square rods (0.22 acres) and was bounded on the east by the East Branch of the Acoaxet River and on the south by land of Joseph Sowle, a distance of 8 3/4 rods, thence north 4 rods and thence east, in a line parallel to the south boundary, to the river. The direction of the south boundary is given as west 7 degrees north and the north boundary is parallel to it, or east 7 degrees south. The deed also granted Paul Cuffe an access way from his wharf along Isaac Sowle's south property line to Drift Way.

Eleven years later, in 1800, Paul Cuffe purchased an adjacent piece of property from Lemuel Sowle, the heir of Joseph Sowle and a first cousin of Isaac Sowle. This new property, carved out of the northeast corner of Lemuel Sowle's homestead, was approximately one-half the size of the previous purchase and thus increased the size of Paul Cuffe's dock and boat works by fifty percent. The combined properties had approximately 50 rods (0.31 acres), being 6 rods (100 ft) north to south and 8 and 3/4 rods (145 ft) east to west. Paul continued to operate out of this property for the rest of his life, and ultimately bequeathed it to two of his children—Rhoda and William. He also most likely had his family residence at this location from 1789 onwards, as discussed below.

## The Eddy Homestead and the Allen Lot

In 1799, Paul Cuffe purchased two large properties from Ebenezer Eddy. One was the Eddy homestead of 100 acres with a dwelling house and ancillary buildings, for which he paid $2,500. The second was a 40-acre parcel, apparently without any buildings, purchased for $1,000. Interestingly, the price was $2.50 per acre in each case. One year later, Paul sold the 100-acre Eddy homestead to his brother-in-law, Michael Wainer (married to Paul's sister, Mary Slocum) for the same price. According to the deed, Michael Wainer and family were already residing on the property. It is our conclusion that Paul Cuffe purchased this property on behalf of his sister and brother-in-law and never intended it for his own use.

The second property of 40 acres was referred to as "the Allen property" or "Allen Lot," and it remained in his possession until his death. Paul Cuffe bequeathed this property to his youngest son, William, along with $300 to build a house for him on the lot. This suggests that there was no suitable dwelling on the Allen lot prior to this time. This property lay to the north of Paul Cuffe's wharf and eventual homestead. It abutted the Acoaxet River on the east and property of Benjamin Soule to the south.

## The "Machine Lot"

Paul Cuffe received the title to the "machine lot" through a mortgage deed from Barnea Devol in August, 1814, shortly before his second trip to Sierra Leone and three years before his death. The "machine lot" was a 46.5-acre parcel bounded by a river known in early times as the "mill river" to the south and east; by the area recently occupied by the Montessori School of the Angels on American Legion Highway to the north; and by lower Forge Road to the west.

The "machine lot" was near one of the earliest settlements in the town. Being located along the westerly side of the river, the area had a long history of water-power related activities. There is a report that at one time a factory that made leather belts to be used in other mills was located there.

While we know Paul Cuffe acquired the title to the "machine lot" in 1814, the property was not listed in the inventory of his real estate compiled by John Mosher, Abner Brownell, and Tillinghast Tripp after his death and submitted to the Judge of Probate, H. Baylies, by the two executors of his will, William Rotch Jr and Daniel Wing, on December 2, 1817. Nor is it mentioned specifically in his will. There is, however, in the inventory of his estate, under notes and obligations, a claim on Barnea Devol for $600, the same amount as in the original deed for the property. This shows clearly that this was a mortgage agreement rather than an intent to acquire the property. After default on the mortgage, the property became part of Paul Cuffe's estate.

### Properties Purchased to Assist Widows of Friends or Relatives

Paul Cuffe, in his late years, provided financial assistance to several widows after their husbands had died. These properties ended up in his possession when he died in September 1817, and were included in his estate inventory and will.

### The "Meeting House Lot" of Catherine Cook

The "Meeting House Lot" refers to a property that Paul Cuffe purchased from the widow Catherine Cook in 1816. She was selling this and another property to raise the funds needed to settle the estate of her late husband, Benjamin Cook. The property surrounded the Allens Neck Meeting House, which is still located at 739 Horseneck Road, in the town of Dartmouth.

In his will, signed April 18, 1817, Paul Cuffe "returned this property to the widow (Catherine Cook) and Benjamin's heirs, they "paying what the land cost and interest." It is not clear whether he meant for them to pay what he had paid for the property in 1816 or some other amount. It is clear from these several actions that Paul Cuffe was essentially helping out the widow and her family, including her son and his son-in-law, Pardon Cook, and his daughter, Alice Cook, and that he owned the property for a very limited period of time.

### The John and Lucy Castino Property

Paul Cuffe's acquisition of the Castino property was somewhat similar in purpose to that of Catherine Cook's Meeting House lot. John Castino, son of Raymond Castino, both mariners, married Lucy Maccumber (Macomber), daughter of Noah Macomber, in June 1807. That same year, the couple purchased a lot of 40 rods from Nathaniel Sowle.

The property abutted the east branch of the Acoaxet River on the east, David Sowle's property on the south, and Nathaniel Sowle's property on the west and north. This David Sowle property was the same four-acre parcel that Paul Cuffe would buy for his homestead in 1813, as described previously. Thus, when Paul Cuffe acquired his homestead land, John and Lucy Castino were the abutters to the north, along the riverfront.

John Castino died, probably in early 1813, and his wife was appointed executor of his estate. On July 13, 1813, Lucy Castino sold this property to Paul Cuffe, who was the highest bidder in a public auction. She retained the right of dower and continued to reside in the house on this property.

In his will, probated in 1818, Paul Cuffe gave to his daughter, Mary Cuffe Phelps, and her heirs and assigns the house and lot of land that he had bought from Lucy Castino. On February 17, 1818, Alvin Phelps, husband of Mary Phelps, purchased Lucy Castino's right of dower to this property.

### The Deborah Sowle Property

Captain Ebenezer Vose Sowle died in May of 1814. In August of 1816, his widow, the administrator of his estate, sold a nine-acre property to Paul Cuffe for $315, probably under a mortgage agreement to help provide funds for the widow.

The property is described as follows: "starting at a heap of stones by the wall in Pardon Kirbys line thence south eleven degrees and a half west about 32 rods to a heap of stones for a corner, thence east twelve degrees south 25 rods and 5 feet to the orchard wall, thence north eight degrees east 7 rods to the northwest corner of the orchard, thence east 18 degrees south 28 rods, 7 feet as the wall stands to Gideon Cornell's land thence north 18 degrees east 23 rods and 10 feet to Pardon Kirby's line, thence west 28 degrees north fourteen rods, thence west 14 degrees north in said Kirby's line to the first mention bounds. So, bounded by Pardon Kirby on the north, and probably the east by Gideon Cornell."

The Deborah Sowle property was located on both sides of Drift Way, approximately one mile south of the Paul Cuffe homestead. This property was inherited by Paul Cuffe's daughter Alice Cuffe Cook, who built a house on the west side of the road.

## Two Salt Meadows Near Horseneck

In 1812, Paul Cuffe and Michael Wainer purchased a salt meadow from Robert Wilcox. It was located in the Horseneck area and adjoined the Let. It was bounded as follows:

> beginning at a stake the edge of the upland, a bound between the meadow of Robert Giffords formerly from thence east forty degrees and half north by a range of stakes to the cove, then we begin again at said stake first mentioned, from thence east eight and twenty degrees south along by the edge of the upland thirty rods and one half to a stake, then southerly and easterly along by the edge of the upland or as the Return gives it, until we come parallel with the northwest corner of Jonathan Gifford's house thence east in the same range to shore or let, so-called. The meadow is bounded easterly on the let, northerly on Giffords, so called, westerly on the upland and southerly on Benjamin Wilcox meadow.

In 1816, Paul Cuffe purchased a second salt meadow in the Horseneck area from Jeffrey Wilcox for $100. It was at a place called "The Opening," and was bounded as follows:

> Northward on the creek, westward on a lot of Salt Meadow now or formerly belonging to William Sanford, southward partly on the Sand Hills and the land formerly belonging to Salburys, easterly on meadow formerly belonging to George Allen now in the possession of the heirs of Benjamin Wilcox and for a more particular description reference may be had of the last will and testament of Joseph Allen in which he gave said lot of Meadow to his son Abner Allen; and said meadow was afterwards conveyed from said Abner to my honoured father William Wilcox of said Westport, deceased, and to his heirs.

## The Windmill at the Point

This property apparently involved a lease of an existing windmill at Acoaxet (Westport) Point by Paul Cuffe, Washington Davis, and Samuel Hicks, from the owners, Philip and Humphrey Macomber, for $120 for as long as they should continue to operate the mill.

The mill was located a little north of Charles Macomber's dwelling house. According to the report on the so-called Benjamin Hicks house at 1865 Main Road, Westport Point, submitted to the Massachusetts Historical Commission, Charles Macomber owned and resided in this house from 1794 to 1805. Thus, the mill was located on the property on the west side of Main Road, north of Cape Bial Lane, now 1853 Main Road. We have not found a record of the later disposition of this windmill by Cuffe, Davis, and Hicks; the length of time they may have operated it; or when it might have been dismantled.

### Cuffe & Howards Store in New Bedford

Lamont Thomas (pp. 41-45) provides an informative discussion of the store that Paul Cuffe was engaged in at the corner of Water Street and Union Street in New Bedford with his two sons-in-law, Peter and Alexander Howard. Both Peter and Alexander were freed slaves, who had worked at Paul Cuffe's boatyard as skilled carpenters on construction of the ship *Alpha* in 1806. Soon thereafter, they married two of Paul and Alice Cuffe's daughters, Naomi (Sarah) and Ruth, and in 1809, they opened Cuffe & Howards store specializing in products from the West Indies.

The property was apparently rented from Seth Russell Sr., who had purchased the land from his father Joseph Russell III. Around 1820, the younger Russell sons, Seth Jr. and Charles, erected the Sundial Building at this location. After Peter Howard's death, his brother Alexander became partners with Richard Johnson. Following Alexander's death, his widow Ruth (Cuffe) married Johnson, who appears to have moved the business to South Water Street in New Bedford.

### The Salt Works

Paul Cuffe entered into an joint business agreement with Joseph Tripp on April 21, 1817, to establish a 2,000-square-foot salt works on the eastern edge of Joseph Tripp's property.

They agreed that the salt works would be developed on land at the easternmost part of Joseph Tripp's farm; that the cost of preparing the facilities would be shared; that Joseph Tripp would be responsible for managing the operation of the salt works; and that he, Tripp, would receive an annual rent of five dollars for the land plus one-fifth of the annual salt production.

This agreement was made only five months before Paul Cuffe's death and seems to suggest that the intention was to start the salt production by the summer of 1817. There is a provision in Paul Cuffe's will that his wife should receive the proceeds from this activity and that, in the event it was not functioning, she should receive an annual sum of one hundred dollars instead. This suggests that the expected income from Paul Cuffe's four-fifths' share of the production might have been a similar amount.

The property on which we believe the salt works was to be located was purchased by Joseph Tripp and his brother, Benajah, in two transactions. The first involved acquisition of a one-acre parcel from John Avery Parker, the wealthy shipbuilder, and his brother-in-law, Levi Standish, on August 22, 1816. The parcel was described as: "beginning at the southeast corner of David Kirby's land by the

Salt Water at the easternmost end of the fence, thence along a wall thence west, 5 degrees north, 13 rods to a stub and stones on the south side of the wall, thence south 5 degrees west a little more than 14 rods to the creek, thence easterly and northerly by the water (creek and river) to the first mentioned bound."

In a deed dated May 30, 1817, Joseph and Benajah Tripp purchased from their father, Caleb Tripp, two abutting parcels extending their original holding to the west and south and still abutting the property of David Kirby to the north. Whether these parcels were linked to the planned salt works is not clear.

It appears that the salt works was never established, however, because the two Tripp Brothers sold this same property, consisting of ten acres, to David Kirby on August 21, 1820 for $950, and there was no mention on the deed of any structures or a salt works existing on the property. The deed does record that David Kirby was the abutter along the north line of the property, westerly on the highway, southerly on the land formerly belonging to David Russell, and easterly on the river.

In 1820, David Kirby was living in the Waite-Kirby-Potter House in present day Central Village, but his land extended down to the east branch of the Westport River. David Russell was living at what later became the Town Farm on Drift Road. Thus, the land owned by Joseph and Benajah Tripp on which a salt works was intended to be constructed in collaboration with Paul Cuffe was on the east branch of the Westport River, somewhat north of the Town Farm.

### The Paul Cuffe School

One reason to believe that Paul Cuffe perhaps had access to the various Sowle properties is that the Paul Cuffe School, which Cuffe reportedly built around

*Early Westport schoolhouse similar to the one Paul Cuffe built, circa 1815.*

*— Painting by Joseph S. Russell, courtesy of the New Bedford Whaling Museum*

1797, seems to have been located on David Sowle's property on the west side of Drift Road, a part of the land David inherited from his father, Isaac Sowle. An 1831 map of Westport shows a school in this area, and several nineteenth-century deeds refer to a "schoolhouse lot" at that point. While the story of the Paul Cuffe School is recorded in many places, we have not been able to establish precisely where it was located.

### Where Was Paul Cuffe's Homestead?

As previously noted, Paul Cuffe purchased a small property of 35 square rods (0.22 acres) on the banks of the east branch of the Acoaxet River, where he established his wharf and boatyard, in 1789. There is no direct evidence that he built a residence there in any of the deeds or property records, but there is indirect evidence from the 1790 census that he and his family were residing in this area. That census listing appears to record households in a sequence reflecting neighbors as though the census-taker had worked his way along a road, such as Drift Way (Drift Road), near which this Cuffe property was located. The names of heads of households preceding the entry for Paul Cuffe (actually recorded as Paul Cuff in the census) and his family of seven are: Lemuel Sowle, Joseph Sowle, Isaac Sowle, and David Sowle. The names following Cuffe are Silvanus Wilcox, Benjamin Sowle, Jacob Sowle, and Daniel Allen. All of the Sowles were immediate neighbors to the south and north of the boatyard property. This suggests strongly that the Cuffe family had their residence in this area.

Unfortunately, the 1800 Westport census lists the heads of households in alphabetical order, so it is impossible to determine who one's neighbors were. The 1810 census lists in the order of domiciles, so it provides better information regarding one's probable neighbors. Among the listings preceding Paul Cuffe (who was again recorded as Paul Cuff, this time with eleven persons in his family) were: Daniel Allen, Green Allen, Humphrey Allen, Sarah Soal (widow of Isaac and mother of David), David Soal, and Weston Allen. These were all neighbors to the north of Paul Cuffe's boatyard. The name following Paul Cuffe was Luthan Tripp, who at that time owned the property to the south of the boatyard. The census-taker had worked his way south on Drift Road.

These census records provide reasonably strong evidence that Paul Cuffe and his family were living in very close proximity to the boat yard from at least 1790 onward, but they are not conclusive. Another source significantly strengthens the case for concluding that he had built a substantial home on the boatyard property. In 1798, the US Congress levied a direct tax on dwelling houses, lands, and slaves, providing assessments of the values of such properties at that time.

According to the tax assessment records, Paul Cuff possessed a dwelling house and outbuildings that were worth $620. This property was worth more than that of either of his neighbors Lemuel or Joseph Sowle and was only slightly less than the $640 valuation of the dwelling house and outbuilding of the very wealthy merchant and shipowner, Isaac Cory, at Westport Point. This Cory house is still standing at 2043 Main Road.

In the 1798 national tax assessment, Paul Cuffe is recorded as the owner of another house in Westport, which was occupied by Barker Little at that time and had an assessed value of $125. It was listed next to the property of John Cuffe, which had a residence with a similar value. Both of these houses were probably located on the farm that Paul and John had inherited from their father, Cuff Slocum.

Other than this farm, the only property that Paul Cuffe owned in 1798 on which the $620-house could have been built was the 0.22-acre property that he had purchased from Isaac Sowle in 1789—the property on which he had established his wharf and boatyard. In 1800, he purchased from Lemuel Sowle a small parcel of 0.11 acres that abutted his boatyard property to the south.

The property that is referred to in Paul Cuffe's will as his homestead was essentially a sizable extension of the property around his wharf and home. The official deed recording the transaction between David Sowle and Paul Cuffe was signed on March 13, 1813. This was land that David Sowle had acquired as part of the settlement of his father Isaac's estate in 1791.

David Soule inherited fourteen acres, which he held for nineteen years before he sold it as three separate pieces to Paul Cuffe (four-plus acres), Luthan Tripp (two acres) and Christopher Russell (seven acres). All three of these transactions were signed within one month, March 13 to April 13, 1813. Paul Cuffe, in his will dated April 18, 1817, divided this homestead property among his six children, with the dwelling house, the dock, and the boatyard being divided between his two youngest children, Rhoda and William.

This Paul Cuffe homestead property is now essentially identical with the two properties at 1430-1436 Drift Road, currently owned by the LaFrance family. It is approximately 500 yards north of the property at 1504 Drift Road that is mistakenly recorded as the Paul Cuffe Farm on the National Register of Historic Places and the Massachusetts Inventory of Historic Places.

In Paul Cuffe's time, that property belonged to Tillinghast Tripp, an immediate neighbor to the north of Michael Wainer. Information on the exact location of the Paul Cuffe boatyard, residence, and homestead is provided in the Appendix section dealing with the property holdings of the Sowle (Soule) family.

## Summing Up

Paul Cuffe purchased or leased property mainly for four purposes:

- To conduct businesses and house his family—boatyard, windmill, West Indies goods store, and homestead
- To help family members acquire property—the Eddy farm and salt marshes with Michael Wainer
- To help widows Lucy Castino, Catherine Cook, and Deborah Sowle meet the obligations of their deceased spouses
- To loan money against mortgaged properties—the "Machine Lot" and the Nathaniel Sowle property

The one property that does not fall easily into these categories is the Allen Lot, purchased in 1799 from Ebenezer Eddy along with the Eddy homestead, which he sold to Michael Wainer the next year. There are no clear records as to whether he used the Allen Lot of forty acres for farming or hired others to farm it, as he apparently did with his share of the family farm on Old County Road. As noted above, he bequeathed the Allen Lot to his youngest son, William, along with a grant of three hundred dollars to build a house on it.

There is no indication that Paul Cuffe purchased property for speculative purposes or made any profit on property purchased and then sold to his brother-in-law, Michael Wainer.

In essence, Paul Cuffe's property acquisitions in and around Westport were either to conduct his principal businesses, house his family, or to help others meet their financial obligations—a practical, generous, public-spirited approach paralleling his efforts to help the people of Sierra Leone achieve economic progress.

## Michael Wainer's Properties

Michael Wainer, alias Micah Quaben, was born about 1748, probably in Aquinnah (formerly Gay Head), Martha's Vineyard or Dartmouth, and was the son of Margaret Waner, alias Quebbin. He recorded his intentions to marry Deborah Pequit in 1769, but apparently she died soon thereafter. He then married her sister, Lydia Pequit, on May 1, 1770. Lydia also died soon after the marriage, and on October 11, 1772 he married Mary Slocum, daughter of Cuff and Ruth (Moses) Slocum, and older sister of Paul Cuffe. That same year, Cuff Slocum died.

## The Russells Mills Property

In 1776, four years after their marriage, Michael and Mary Wainer purchased property near the intersecting roadways that form the center of Russells Mills Village. The village was built around the convergence of the Paskamansett (or Slocum) River and Destruction Brook, where a number of fulling, grist and other mills tapped the water power generated by the streams. The Wainers purchased the three-quarter-acre property from Giles Russell, a clothier, who had a fulling mill alongside one of the streams and was a member of one of Dartmouth's and New Bedford's founding families.

A summary of the property description in the deed is as follows:

*For £ 3, 6s, for a tract of land in Dartmouth near my fulling mill lying in the fork or parting of the ways containing 3/4 acre, bounded as follows: beginning at a heap of stones in the south line of the way that leads by my house to Allens neck, said heap of stones is north 35 degrees east 8 1/4 rods from Michael Wainers dwelling house standing on the premises. Thence from said stone heap south 22 degrees east ten rods to another stone heap, thence south 25 degrees west about 3 1/2 rods to the other way leading out of Smiths Neck by the mills, the foregoing lines divides it off from the remainder of my land, all other ways bounded by said ways leading of the said neck. The premises with the buildings thereon and their appurtenances and stand seized thereof etc.*

This is the triangular property on which Devoll's General Store in Dartmouth is currently located. In her book, Beverly Glennon lists Michael Wainer as the first owner of the property on which that store, later owned by the Glennons, is located.

It is clear that there was a dwelling house on the lot when the Wainers purchased it. At the time, Michael Wainer was a cordwainer or tanner, tanning leather for shoes, belts, breeches and saddles. Although Glennon writes that there were tanneries on Tannery Lane, which abuts the Wainer property on the south, she does not list him as one of the people engaged in the area's tanning industry. Nonetheless, it seems likely that he was operating a tannery there between 1776 and 1792.

On April 7, 1792, Michael and Mary Wainer sold the land and the dwelling to Dartmouth merchant William Howland for 15 pounds. Mary surrendered all her right and power of thirds (dower) in relation to the premises.

## Farm Properties in Westport, 1789-1799

Between 1789 and 1799, Michael Wainer acquired eight properties. Two of these were purchased in 1792 and 1793 from Holder Slocum's sons Christopher and Holder Jr. These properties were part of larger farm holdings owned by the Holder Slocum family. Holder Sr. and, subsequently, his two sons also owned the western Elizabeth Islands, including Cuttyhunk, where the Cuff Slocum family lived from 1751 to 1767 and where Michael Wainer's wife, Mary, grew up.

The first seven of the properties listed below were inside an area bounded on the north by Hix Bridge Road, on the west by Horseneck Road, on the east by Fisher Road, and on the south by a line extending Cross Road to the west. The sixth and seventh properties on the list were actually a 25-acre parcel on the south side of Hix Bridge Road between Horseneck and Division Roads that was owned by two related families, Cook and Cornell. There is no indication in the deed that there were any structures on these properties. The eighth property on the list was a 12.5-acre woodlot on the west side of Fisher Road in Dartmouth that he purchased in 1799.

The currencies recorded in the several deeds are noteworthy, especially since all these transactions took place after the establishment of the United States and the introduction of the US dollar as the currency of the country. Four of the transactions dating from 1789 to 1799, were recorded in English pounds. Three transactions dating from 1796 to 1799 were paid in US dollars, and one, in 1797, was paid in silver dollars, denoting Spanish milled silver dollars. This suggests that the US dollar was still not well established or accepted as the currency of the land even up to two decades after independence.

After he acquired his homestead property in 1800, purchased from Paul Cuffe as described in the previous section, Michael Wainer sold all these eight properties to two of his sons. So, in a way, they are of transient interest, having been a part of his assets during the decade of the 1790s but then passed on to his sons.

Michael Wainer had eight sons and two daughters. Six of those sons were active seamen; two others, Gardner and David, were farmers. It may well have been that during the period from 1792, when he sold the property at Russells Mills, until 1800, when he acquired the Eddy homestead, Michael was moving his investments from shipping into farmland, which he later sold to two of his sons.

### Excerpts from Eight Property Deeds

- 1789, April 13, Edward Wing of Dartmouth, yeoman, to Michael Wainer of Dartmouth, NBRD, Book 12, p. 127:

  *"An Indian man" for £25 4 s. land in Dartmouth (sic), a "part of the land that I bought of William Ricketson," 9 acres, beginning in the north line of John Ricketson then east 17 degrees north 32 rods, then north 5.25 rods to David Wing, then west in Wing's line 39 rods, then 42rods on a straight line to the point of beginning.*

- 1792, April 4, Chistopher Slocum to Micel (Michael) Wainer, NBRD, Book 12, p. 533:

  *For £14 8s. paid by Mical Wainer of Dartmouth Mariner, 8 acres situated in Dartmouth, bounded as follows: beginning at the southwest corner of Samuel Macombers land, being also the northwest corner of this lot and thence south seven degrees and three quarters east in John Ricketsons line about 86 rods to a stake for the southwest corner thence east 7 degrees north about 15 rods to a stake for a southeast corner then begin again at Samuel Macombers corner first mentioned thence east seven degrees and a half north in said Macombers line about 15 rods to a stake for a northeast corner thence south seven degrees and 3/4 east parallel with the westerly line till it comes to the southeasterly corner aforementioned. bounded westerly on John Ricketson's land southerly on Jonathan Gifford's land easterly on my own land, northerly on Samuel Macomber's land."*

  Witnesses Christopher Slocum 2nd and Benj Russell.
  Recorded 21 April 1793.

  Note that in this deed, Michael Wainer is identified as a "mariner," whereas in most of the subsequent deeds he is identified as a "yeoman." At the time of this purchase, Michael and Paul Cuffe were commanding the ships that they jointly owned.

- 1793, Holder Slocum to Michael Wainer, NBRD, Book 13, p. 269:

  *Holder Slocum of Dartmouth, yeoman, for £25 10s, paid by Michael Wainer of Dartmouth, Mariner, a parcel of land situated in Westport, bounded off at the southwesterly corner of my land joining to Edward Wings land in manner following, beginning at the corner of the wall the southwest corner of my land thence north seven degrees and a half west thirty three rods and nine feet to a corner of the wall thence east seven degrees and a half north five rods and five feet to a stake, thence south seven degrees and a half east thirty three rods and nine feet to a stake in the south line of my land, thence on a strait line to the bound first mentioned.*

  25 January 1793, recorded 16 April 1794.
  Holder and Abigail Slocum
  Witnesses Edward Slead, Ackurs (sic) Sisson.

The tract contains five acres and 48 rods. (This appears to be the southwest corner of the Holder Slocum land that abutted Edward Wing's land on the west and Holder Slocum's land on the north and east. No indication of who is to the south.)

- 1796, Samuel and Comfort Wilcox to Michael Wainer. NBRD, Book 14, p. 107:

*Samuel Wilcox of Westport, yeoman and wife Comfort for $280 to Michael Waner, Yeoman of Westport, "part of the homestead farm of William Ricketson of Dartmouth, late of Dartmouth, deceased," 21 acres and 33 rods, beginning at the southeast corner of Michael Wainer, then south 27 rods then west 13.5 degrees south 25.5 rods, then west 40 degrees south 7 rods, then west 16 degrees north 25 rods, then west 21.5 degrees north 9.75 rods then north 11 degrees west 3.25 rods, then north 45 rods and 20 feet to David Wing's line, then east 42 rods to Wainer's line, then east 17 degrees north 25 rods and 11 feet to the point of beginning.*

*Bounded east and south by Isaac Lawrence, west by Edward Wing, North by David Wing and Michael Wainer. The deed was executed March 24, 1796. This is part of the parcel of 33 acres and 33 rods conveyed in 1806 by Michael Wainer to Gardner Wainer.*

- 1797, John Wing to Michael Wainer. NBRD, Book 14, p. 374:

*John Wing of Dartmouth, yeoman, for 166.67 Silver Dollars, paid by Michael Waner of Westport, yeoman, a tract of land situated in Westport containing 10 acres, bounded as follows, beginning at a small rock in the line of John Cornells land and about 58 rods easterly from Jerathman (sic) Whites north east corner of his land, thence south 2 degrees east 29 rods and 1/2 to a maple tree standing in the line of John Fishers land, thence east 8 degrees north 54 rods to a tree marked thence north 2 degrees west 33 rods to a heap of stones, thence west 10 degrees south 54 rods to the bound first mentioned. Bounded north on Cornells land, west on John Wings land south on John Fishers land in part and part on Parden Cornells land, easterly on said Wings own land. – 2 Feb. 1797.*

- 1799, John Cornell to Michael Wainer. NBRD, Book 15, p. 167:

*For £15 s6 a tract of land in Westport containing 4 1/4 acres, bounded as follows: beginning at the corner of the wall Bennet Cooks southwest corner thence south 2 degrees west six rods to a stake, thence east 22 degrees south five rods and four feet to a stake, thence east 37 degrees north 57 1/4 rods to a stake for a corner thence north 30 degrees west ten rods to said Bennet Cook's land thence westerly in his line to the bound first mentioned. Bounded east and south on John Cornells land, west on Jacob Tripps land and north on Bennett Cooks land.*

> – 17 January 1799 John and Mehitable Cornell
> Witnesses: Paul Wainer, Rhoda Wainer

- 1799, Bennett Cook to Michael Wainer. NBRD, Book 15, p.168:

*"For $500 a parcel of land of 20 acres in Westport, bounded as follows: Beginning at a heap of stones on the south side of the highway thence south 28 degrees east 13 rods and 6 feet to a stake, thence east 30 degrees north until it comes to the wall on*

*Thomas Cornells line, thence north as the wall stands until it comes to the highway, thence west as the highway goes until it comes to the first mentioned bound.*

*Bounded as follows: west on Jacob Tripps land, southerly partly on Bennett Cooks land the he bought of John Cornell and part on John Cornells land. East on Thomas Cornells land, northerly on the highway.*

> – 17 January 1799. Bennett Cook and Experience Cook
> Witnesses: Holder Russell, Joel Packard, John Cornell, Pardon Cornell

This property and the previous property of John Cornell were abutting properties and probably part of a joint transaction. Bennett Cook and John Cornell were related by marriage. Michael Wainer subsequently sold the two properties to his son Thomas Wainer.

- 1799, Abraham and Stephen Gifford to Michael Wainer. NBRD. Book 16, p. 169:

*Giffords both of Dartmouth, for $75 by Michael Wainer, Blackman of Westport, yeoman, a lot of woodland of 12 1/2 acres, in Dartmouth, bounded as follows: beginning at a black oak tree on the westerly side of the highway leading by Fisher's, thence north 16 degrees and 1/4 west 47 rods to a stake on the westerly side of said way thence south 40 degrees west 59 rods to a maple tree standing beside a brook, thence south 16 degrees and 1/4 east 42 rods to a stake in Allens line, thence east about 45 degrees north 59 rods to the bound first mentioned. Bounded east on the highway, northerly on Cornell and Cooks land, westerly on said Giffords own land, southerly on land belonging to Elizabeth Allen.*

> – 23 January 1799.
> Witnesses: Thomas Gifford, Job Gifford
> Recorded: 18 April 1799.

## Acquiring the Eddy Homestead from Paul Cuffe, 1800

As described previously, Paul Cuffe bought the 100-acre Ichabod Eddy/Ebenezer Eddy homestead a few hundred yards south of his boatyard/residence in 1799 and then sold it to his brother-in-law and sister the following year for the same $2,500. According to the deed, the Wainers were already residing on the property in 1800, which gives the impression that Paul Cuffe purchased this large farm on the west bank of the Acoaxet River for his close relative and partner, with the understanding that they would pay him for it when they were able.

The key provisions of the deed were as follows:

- 1800, March 17. Paul Cuffe to Michael Wainer, 100 ac. $2,500. NBRD, Book 16, p. 390:

*The farm where said Michael Wainer now lives, that I bought of Ebenezer Eddy, in Westport on the west side of the east branch of Acoaxet River. Bounded easterly partly on land belonging to the heirs of Isaac Sowle, partly on land belonging to Lemuel Sowle, partly on Lemuel Tripp's land and partly on said river. Southerly partly on Daniel Tripp's land and partly on John Davis's land, westerly partly on William Macomber's land, and partly on land belonging to ye heirs of Stephen Sowle. Northerly partly on William Kirby's land, partly on Lemuel Sowle's land*

*and partly on Daniel Tripp's land. All
the rights and privileges except the
privilege that the heirs of Stephen Sowle
has to pass through a part of said farm,
and ye privilege that John Davis has to
pass through a part of said farm, and
excepting ye burying ground on said farm
reserved by said Ebenezer Eddy.*

Wainer Homestead, 1510 Drift Road,
Westport.– *Spinner Publications Archives*

This became the homestead of the
Wainer family, parts of which have
subsequently passed down through the generations. The house was torn down in
1974 by John E. Roberts. A photo of the house is shown in the Appendix.

### Selling Smaller Farm Properties to Michael Wainer's Sons

After acquiring the Eddy property for his own homestead, Michael Wainer
sold off the seven smaller properties that he had acquired in 1790s to two of his
sons, Thomas and Gardner. A summary of these transactions is as follows:

- 1800, Michael Wainer to Thomas Wainer, NBRD, Book 16, p. 389:
  *For $600, for 3 tracts of land:
  20 acres bought of Bennett Cook;
  4 1/4 acres bought of John Cornell
  12 1/2 acres woodlot in Dartmouth bought of Abraham and Stephen Gifford*

- 1806, Michael Wainer to Gardiner Wainer, NBRD, Book18, p. 2:
  *Michael Wainer of Westport, Yeoman, for $800 paid by Gardiner Wainer of Westport,
  Mariner. A tract of land in Westport and is part of which I bought of Edward Wing and
  part of Samuel Willcox, late of Westport, deceased, containing 33 acres and 33 rods.
  Bounded north by David Wing, east by Joseph Wing and Thomas Shermans land.*

- 1806, Michael Wainer to Gardner Wainer, NBRD, Book 17, p. 500:
  *$200 for land in Westport being part of that I bought of Holder Slocum and part of
  Christopher Slocum of Dartmouth, deceased, contains 13 acres and 48 rods.*

### Later Additions of Farming Land by Michael Wainer

As mentioned in Part 2, Michael Wainer and Paul Cuffe jointly purchased a
salt meadow in the area near Horseneck and the so-called "Let" in the Westport
River. It is not clear what Paul Cuffe's interest in this property was, as there is
no indication that he was raising livestock, but Michael Wainer probably was,
and Paul may have just joined him in the venture. A summary of the deed is as
follows:

- 1812 Robert Wilcox sold a salt meadow to Paul Cuffe and Michael Wainer
  for $210. NBRD, Book 21, p. 129:
  *Situate lying and being in the Horse neck, and adjoining the let, so called, beginning
  at a stake the edge of the upland, a bound between the meadow of Robert Giffords
  formerly from thence east forty degrees and half north by a range of stakes to the*

*cove, then we begin again at said stake first mentioned, from thence east eight and twenty degrees south along by the edge of the upland thirty rods and one half to a stake, then southerly and easterly along by the edge of the upland or as the Return gives it, until we come parallel with the northwest corner of Jonathan Gifford's house thence east in the same range to shore or let, so-called. The meadow is bounded easterly on the let, northerly on Giffords, so called, westerly on the upland and southerly on Benjamin Wilcox meadow.*

The following year, Michael Wainer purchased a small, irregular piece of farmland that abutted the southwest corner of his homestead farm from Charles Derrow as follows:

- 1813 Charles Derrow to Michael Wainer, NBRD, Book 21, p. 330:
  *Charles Derrow of Westport for $202, paid by Michael Wainer of Westport yeoman, 5 acres 126 rods beginning at a corner of a wall thence west 15 degrees north forty one rods, thence south 15 degrees and 1/2 east six and 1/2 rods thence south 3 degrees west 18 rods thence east 15 degrees south 38 rods, thence north 7 degrees east 24 rods to the first mentioned bound, bounded westerly and southerly on John Davis land, easterly and northerly on the said Wainer's land.*
  – 4 June, 1813, recorded 28 April, 1814.

Michael Wainer died on August 4, 1815, and on October 29, 1816, Paul Cuffe was appointed executor of his will. Because Paul had been away on his last trip to Sierra Leone from December of 1815 to July of 1816, the executor responsibilities for Michael Wainer's estate were taken over by Anselm Bassett, Adam Gifford, and Daniel Wing.

In his will, Michael Wainer bequeathed to his widow, Mary White Wainer, and his last son, Rodney, the main farm house and land on both sides of Drift Way for their use and improvement until Rodney attained the age of 21. Eldest son Thomas received land on the east side of Drift Way at or near the southeast corner. Son Michael Wainer Jr. received land at the northwest section of the farm, and son Paul received land on the west side of Drift Way, bordering with Luthan Tripp to the north.

### Summing Up Michael Wainer

Michael Wainer and Paul Cuffe were related by marriage and were close friends and partners in many ventures. Five of Michael and Mary Wainer's sons were ship captains who sailed on and captained ships owned by Michael and Paul. Paul's sister, Mary Slocum Wainer, died in 1804; Michael married Mary White in 1806, and they had one son, Rodney, in 1807.

A familial connection with the Michael and Mary Wainer homestead has been maintained over the years. Their descendants still own parts of the old farm property and recall visits to an old farmhouse on the west side of Drift Road when they were young. The property is now heavily overgrown with invasive plants and trees, but there is a burial plot surrounded by walls, some foundations, a fiberglass hull of an old sloop bearing the name "Wainer Truth" with a 1988 Massachusetts registration, and other testimonies to the legacy of this family.

# Appendix A – Previous Owners of Cuffe and Wainer Properties

As part of an effort to identify the various properties in Westport and Dartmouth that were owned by Paul Cuffe and his brother-in-law, Michael Wainer, we have searched through the deeds and wills to trace the prior owners back to the original purchases by the Plymouth Proprietors from the Wampanoag People. There are three families that we found to be of particular importance in this research—the Sowles, the Eddys, and the Allens. In the following sections we trace these three families' holdings.[63]

### Properties of the Sowles in Dartmouth—17th, 18th, and early 19th Centuries

George Sowle (ca. 1594-1680) was a passenger on the Mayflower and one of the 35 original proprietors of Dartmouth (Dartmouth Proprietary) who received one share (or 1/35th) of the distribution of 70,000 acres purchased from the Wampanoags in 1652. He lived and died in Duxbury, but he was one of the few original proprietors who did not sell off his share. He passed his share to two of his sons, Nathaniel and George.

In the Dartmouth Proprietors Land Records, there is the following entry:

*George Sowles share...all that belongs to George Sowle share is yet in the Sowle hand or possession only 44 acres sold to Eleazer Slocum. To Nath. Sowle 1/2 of p(ro-prietor')s share bearing date Jan. 22, 1658.*

George Sowle divided his share in the Dartmouth Proprietary in 1658 between his two sons, Nathaniel (1637-1702) and George (1639-1704), who settled in Dartmouth and raised their families. Nathaniel's sons, Nathaniel, Silvanus, and Jacob (a fourth son, Miles, may have been mentally or physically handicapped), and George's sons, William and Nathan, and his daughter Mary's husband, Joseph Devol, received parts of the original land owned by George Sowle. In 1708, they set out the boundaries of each person's property. (See deed transcription, pp. 92–94)

Interestingly, in the 1708 division, the homesteads or probable dwelling places of three of these offspring were identified as follows:

- William[2] Sowle (son of George[1]), west side of the Paskamansett River.
- Nathaniel[2] Sowle (son of Nathaniel[1]), west side of the Acoaxet River.
- Nathan[2] Sowle (son of George[1]), west side of the Acoaxet River.

There is no mention of a homestead or dwelling place for Jacob, Silvanus, or Miles Sowle. In the division, Nathaniel's sons were granted properties next to William's homestead on the Paskamansett River, and George's sons were given some properties on the Acoaxet River.

There were three large properties shown as belonging to the Sowles on the Crane maps of the west side of the east branch of the Acoaxet—now Westport—River. Two are roughly rectangular and the third is shaped like a slice of pie, with the broad end along the bank of the river and the narrow end up near what is now Main Road. The southern parcel is recorded as 132 acres belonging to Nathaniel[3] Soule (Nathaniel[2], George[1]) on Feb. 25, 1742–43. The middle parcel went to George's son Nathan[3] (George[2], George[1]), who passed it on to his two sons, John[4] and Timothy[4] (Nathan[3], George[2], George[1]), and they are recorded as the owners of 129 acres as of March 22, 1742-43 on the Crane maps. The northern parcel went to Jacob[3] Soule (Nathaniel[2], George[1]) (1687–1747-48) and consisted of 145 acres.

The Jacob Soule property (homestead), as shown on the Crane maps, had a northern boundary recorded as East 10° north, and the south boundary as East 17° south. Thus, there was a 27° difference in the boundaries of the pie. These radial lines were carried over into many of the subsequent divisions of this property and are helpful in identifying which properties were part of the Jacob Soule homestead.

Jacob Soule divided his property among his four surviving sons, Joseph (1710/11-1793), Nathaniel (1717/18-1769), Benjamin (1719-1803), and Stephen (1726/7-1789). Stephen received the western tip of the pie, Joseph the southern portion, Nathaniel the middle portion, and Benjamin the northern portion.

*Property holdings on the Noquochoke River, circa 1714 (see Endnotes).*

*Illustration by Raymond C. Shaw; based on Crane Maps*

Nathaniel[4] Sowle had only one son, Isaac[5] (1742-1791), who inherited his father's farm. It was Isaac Sowle who sold to Paul Cuffe the first segment of his wharf in 1789, a 35-rod parcel cut out of the southeast corner of his homestead property on the bank of the east branch of the Westport River.

After Isaac died, his property was divided among his wife, Sarah, and four children: David, b. 1766, Nathaniel b. 1772, Martha b. 1769, and Phebe b, 1778. An 1813 deed records that David Sowle sold to Paul Cuffe a parcel of more than four acres adjacent to his wharf, which became Paul's homestead.

Joseph Sowle (1710/11-1793) also had only one son who grew to maturity, Lemuel (1745-1814), and it was he who sold a second parcel of 15 rods to Paul Cuffe in 1800, which increased the size of the latter's wharf area on the Westport River by about fifty percent to 50 square rods or 0.31 acres.

Between 1796 and 1802, there were a number of property transactions involving various Sowles or those who bought property from Sowles and then resold those properties within a year or two. A list of these transactions is presented below:

*Soule and Allen Family Properties along East Branch of the Acoaxet River, 1725-1750,*

*Illustration by Raymond C. Shaw; based on Crane Maps*

## Sowle Property Sales from 1796 to 1802

- 1796 Book 13, p. 554. *Benjamin Sowle to Lemuel Sowle, $2,225: 66 acres, home-stead farm of Benjamin Sowle.*

  *Bounded east on the river, south on land belonging to the heirs of Isaac Sowle, west on land of the heirs of Ichabod Eddy and north on land of Ebenezer Eddy and Wesson Kirby.*

This 66-acre farm was south of the southern boundaries of the current properties at 1301 Drift (west of the road) and 1314 Drift (east of the road). Benjamin Sowle had no sons, and the purchaser was his nephew Lemuel Sowle.

- 1800 Book 15, p. 477. *Lemuel Sowle to Paul Cuffe (south third of Paul Cuffe's wharf), $16:* 16 rods (0.10 acres) located at the northeast corner of the Lemuel Sowle homestead

  *Beginning at the southwest corner of said Paul Cuffe's lot which is about 8 rods from the river, thence southerly in the same course with the west line of the said Cuff's lot as the fence now stands, 2 rods [33 feet] to a corner, thence easterly as the fence now stands on a line parallel with the south line of the said Cuffe land to the river. The lot is bounded easterly on the river, southerly and westerly on the grantor's own land and northerly on the said Cuffe's own land. And the said*

Soule and Eddy property holdings on the East Branch of Acoaxet River, 1770-1780.

*Illustration by Raymond C. Shaw; based on Crane Maps*

*Paul Cuff agrees to make and maintain at his own expense a good and lawful fence around the whole of said lot that adjoins the said Lemuel Sowle's land.*

- 1801 Book 16, p. 36. *Lemuel Sowle to Robert Earl, $100: 25 acres.*
  *Beginning at northeast corner of land sold to John Davis, then north as the wall stands 36 rods [594 feet] to Paul Cuff's land, then west in Paul Cuff's and Wesson Kirby's line to the northeast corner of Michael Wainer, then south along Michael Wainer's line to the northwest corner of John Davis, then east to the point of beginning. Bounded east on Luthan Tripps property, north on Paul Cuff and William Kirby's properties, west on Michael Wainer's property and south on John Davis's property.*

The Paul Cuffe land that this deed refers to is the Allen Lot, and the Michael Wainer land is the western part of his homestead, formerly the Eddy homestead. This is also the western part of the Benjamin Sowle property that Lemuel Sowle purchased in 1796.

- 1801 Book 16, p. 42. *Lemuel Sowle to Humphrey Howland, $3360: 66 acres,* homestead farm of Lemuel Sowle.
  *Bounded south on Daniel Tripp's and Michael Wainer's properties, west on Michael Wainer's property, north on the property of the heirs of Isaac Sowle and east on Paul Cuff's property and the river.*

This farm centered on the farmhouse now in ruins at 1461 Drift Road. Lemuel Sowle inherited this house from his father, Joseph, who built it circa 1750. In the WHC Inventory, it is mistakenly identified as the house of Benjamin Sowle, who, as stated above, lived some distance north on a farm of equal acreage. The will of Joseph Sowle provided for the establishment of a family cemetery, likely the "Tillinghast Tripp" cemetery along the west side of Drift to the south of the house, and Joseph and his wife probably account for two of the unmarked stones in the front row. Quaker records note that Benjamin Sowle and his wife are buried on the Joseph Sowle farm as well.

The following year, Humphrey Howland sold this property to Daniel, Luthan, and Tillinghast Tripp by deed registered in Book 18, p. 496-7, NBRD. All three of these Tripps were immediate neighbors and close friends of Paul Cuffe and Michael Wainer.

- 1801 Book 16, p. 49. *Lemuel Sowle to Raimon Castino, 46 rods for $30:*
  *Beginning at Wesson Allen's northeast corner bound from thence westerly in said Wesson's line 12 rods 4 ft to Wesson's northwest corner bounds from thence North one degree east four rods to a stake with stones about it from thence east four degrees north to ye wall thence as said wall runs to the river. Right to pass and repass on grantors land to driftway. Must make and maintain a lawful fence. Abutters: Lemuel Sowle on North and West, river on East and Wesson Allen on South.*

- 1801 Book 16, p. 51. *Lemuel Sowle to John Davis, 25 rods [sic; actually 25 acres]:*
  *Beginning at Daniel Tripps's southwest corner, then north 13.00" west by Tripp 36 rods [594 feet], then west 6.30" south 66 rods [1089 feet], then south 12.00" east along Wainer's line until it meets the northwest corner of the Isaac Sowle heirs, then east along the line of Isaac Sowle's heirs to the point of beginning, bounded east*

on property of Daniel Tripp, north property of Lemuel Sowle, westerly on Michael Wainer's property and southerly on property belonging to the heirs of Isaac Sowle.

- 1801 Book 16, p. 54. *Lemuel Sowle to Daniel Tripp*, $600: 11.5 acres. *Beginning at the river then west 7.00" south 50 rods [825 feet], then south 13.00" east 36 rods [594 feet], then east to Wesson Allen's southwest corner, then north to the northwest corner of Raimon Castino, then east to the river, bounded north and west on Lemuel Sowles's property, south on the property of Raimon Castino and the heirs of Isaac Sowle and easterly on property of Raimon Castino, Wesson Allen and the river.*

- 1801 Book 16, p. 54. *Lemuel Sowle to Luthan Tripp*, $600: 12.5 acres. *Beginning at the river, then west 7.00" south 50 rods [825 feet] to a wall west of the driftway, then north 13.00" west along that wall 36 rods [594 feet] to Paul Cuffe's line, then east along Cuffe's line to David Allen's northwest corner, then south 13.00" east 4 rods and 2 feet [68 feet] to Allen's southwest corner, then east 11.30" north along Allen's line to the river, bounded north on property of Paul Cuffe and David*

Division of the Isaac Soule estate among his heirs in 1807, showing the cross-hatched segment that was transferred by David Soule to Paul Cuffe in 1813.

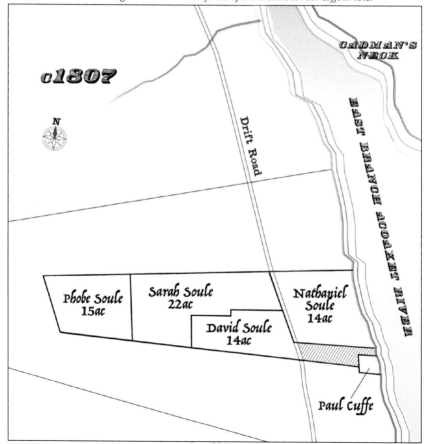

Illustration by Raymond C. Shaw; based on Crane Maps

Allen, easterly on property of David Allen and the river, southerly on property of
Daniel Tripp and westerly on property of Lemuel Sowle.

- 1801 Book 16, p. 55. *Lemuel Sowle to Wesson Allen $30:* 46 rods,
  *Beginning at northeast corner of Isaac Sowle heirs, then west 11 rods and 12 feet
  [192.5 feet] to Allen's cross wall, then north 1.00" east 4 rods and 1 foot [67 feet],
  then east 4.00" north along the wall to the river, bounded east by the river, south by
  property of Isaac Sowle's heirs, west property of Lemuel Sowle and north property
  of Raimon Castino.*

- 1801 Book 16, p. 56. *Lemuel Sowle to David Allen, $34:* 48 rods [0.3 acres],
  *Beginning at Paul Cuffe's southeast corner, then west 12 rods and 12 feet [210 feet]
  to a cross wall, then south 13 degrees east 4 rods and 2 feet, then east 11.30 degrees
  north to the river, bounded north on property of Paul Cuffe, east by the river, south
  and west by the property of Luthan Tripp.*

## Division of the Estate of Isaac Sowle in 1807

- 1807 Book 18, p. 432.

  *Division of the estate of Isaac Sowle, 66 acres, bounded north by property of John
  Davis and Daniel Tripp, east by the river, south by property of Paul Cuffe, Luthan
  Tripp and Tillinghast Tripp, and west by property of Michael Wainer.*

  *1st parcel: To widow, Sarah Sowle. 22 acres, bounded north by John Davis, east by
  Nathaniel Sowle, south by David Sowle and Luthan Tripp, west by Phebe Sowle
  Anthony. Beginning at northwest corner of meadow adjoining east side of highway
  at corner of Daniel Tripp, then S 13.00' E 31 rods and 3 feet [514.5 feet] to a corner of
  a stone wall; W 5.00' N 33 rods [544.5 feet] to a corner; S 8.00" Wt 3 rods [49.5 feet];
  W 90.00' 21 rods [346.5 feet] to the northwest corner of a meadow; South to Luthan
  Tripp's line; West along Tripp's line 40 rods [660 feet]; North to John Davis; East
  along Davis' line to the point of beginning.*

  *2nd parcel: to son, David Sowle: Beginning at a rock on the river at the Nathaniel
  Sowle SE corner, then W 3.00' S to a heap of stones by a wall on the west side of the
  driftway at the SW corner of Nathaniel Sowle , then N 21.00' W 19 rods [313.5 feet],
  then W 5.00' S 33 rods [544.5 feet], then S 8.00' W 3 rods [49.5 feet] [this is notch still
  visible on the north boundary of 1415 Drift], then South to Tripp's line, then East
  to Paul Cuffe's land [at the junction of the Lemuel Sowle lot NW corner and Isaac
  Sowle lot SE corner] Bounded E on the river, S on Paul Cuffe and Luthan Tripp, W
  on Sarah Sowle, N and E on Nathaniel Sowle*

  *3rd parcel to son, Nathaniel Sowle: beginning at Daniel Tripp's boundary at the
  river, then W 49 rods [808.5 feet] to the NW corner of a meadow on the east side
  of the driftway, then S 15.00' E 31 rods and 3 feet [514.5 feet], then S 20.00' E 19 rods
  [313.5 feet] to a heap of stones for a southwest corner, then E 3.00' N to a rock by
  the river. Bounded east on the river, south on David Sowle, west on David Sowle
  and Sarah Sowle and north on Daniel Tripp.*

  *4th parcel to daughter, Phebe Sowle Anthony: the remaining part of the Isaac Sowle
  homestead consisting of 15 acres at the west end of the property.*

## Sale of Property by David Sowle to Paul Cuffe in 1813

In 1813, David Sowle sold to Paul Cuffe a portion of his inherited property running from Drift Way down to the river. Paul Cuffe's wharf, boatyard, and home were at the southeast corner of this property, which consisted of more than four acres, adding to the property what would become Paul Cuffe's homestead. It is not known whether this transaction was merely recognizing a condition that had existed for some years, i.e., Paul Cuffe had been using this area as part of his wharf and home, or if it actually opened up this area to his ownership and use. Paul Cuffe's relationship with the various members of the Isaac Sowle family was so extensive, and probably so close, that either sequence is possible. The map on the previous page shows a hatched area that was formally transferred from David Sowle to Paul Cuffe in 1813.

## Deed on Division of Property of Nathaniel and George Soul [Sowle]

- 1708, 14 May, NBRD, Book 1, Pp 259-60. Division of property of George Soul and sons Nathaniel and William among Nathaniel, Silvanus, Jacob, William, Miles, Nathan Soul, and son-in-law, Joseph Devol (husband of Mary Soul.)

*To all people to whom these presents shall come, Nathaniel Soul, Silvanus Soul and Jacob Soul, Sons of Nathaniel Soul late of Dartmouth in the county of Bristol in new england, and William Soul and Nathan Soul, sons of George Soul late of Dartmouth aforesaid, and brother to said Nathaniel deceased, and Joseph Devol, son in law of said George Soul, all of Dartmouth aforesaid, send greetings. And know ye that whereas said Nathaniel Soul, Silvanus Soul, Jacob Soul, William Soul, Nathan Soul and Joseph Devol being owners and proprietors of several tracts of land within the township of Dartmouth, which did belong to our honored fathers, Nathaniel Soul and George Soul, aforesaid and is all the divided land belonging to their share of land which was given them by their father George Soul late of Duxbury, deceased, by deeds under his hand and seal and is bounded and laid out as by the Purchasers Book of Records, differences thereunto being had may appear and the said land having never yet been divided amongst us according to our rights therein, We do by these presents for the mutual good of us our heirs executors, administrators and assigns and that there may be peace between us and them forever, agree to divide and part and have by these presents divided, parted and set out to each of us and our heirs and assigns forever each one his several parts and proportions according to each of our rights in said tracts of land above said. Hereby binding ourselves, our heirs and assigns to abide by said agreement and division forever in manner following, that is to say:*

*First, on the west side of Pascomanset River where William Soul now liveth, we set out Silvanus Soul's part and proportion to be divided by a line parallel with the line between this land and the land of Peleg Slocum and to be fifty-two Rods wide below and next the River and to continue said parallel being west 1 degree southerly through the lott all on the north side of said line to be Silvanus Soul's part.*

*Secondly on the southerly side of said lott we set for Nathaniel Soul, Jacob and Miles Soul above said, the southerly part of said lott to be parted from the rest in manner* following that is to say to begin at a white oak tree which is a bound of said lott of land and to run north 19 degrees 1/2 westerly 2 rods and 1/2 to a stake by the marsh and from thence to run west 19 degrees and 1/2 southerly through the lott to the road. All on the southerly side of said line to belong to said Nathaniel, Jacob and Miles and further we have set out and divided unto the said Nathaniel, Jacob and Miles all the upland between the last mentioned line and the salt marsh meadow that lies below the swamp or bog joining to the meadow with so much of the said swamp as to take in part of the water that is in said swamp and near the meadow with one rod wide of upland on the west side of said swamp for a conveniency to come to said water.

Thirdly all the remainder of said lott on the west side of Pascomanset River to William Soul.

Fourthly we set out and parted unto said William Soul the southerly part of the land that lies on the west side of Coaxet River where the said Nathaniel and Nathan Soul now dwell to be parted from the rest as follows: to begin at the northwesterly corner of that parcell of land supposed to belong to Increase Allen at a stake which is a bound of our said land and is from the land of William Woods 140 rod distant on a north 16 degrees easterly course and from said stake to run on the same course, viz. north 16 deg. easterly 87 rods & 1/3 to a stake and from thence to run west 16 degrees northerly across the lott unto the line at the Road. All on the southerly side of said line to belong to said William Soul.

Fifthly, we have set out and parted unto the above said Nathaniel Soul, Jacob Soul, Miles Soul that part whereon the said Nathaniel Soul now lives to be divided and parted from the rest in manner following, viz. to begin at a heap of stones below the now dwelling house of said Nathaniel Soul, which is reputed to be an ancient bound erected by our fathers aforesaid for a dividing bound between their land and to run south 17degrees westerly 119 rods 14 yards for the width of this part and home to said Allens land, then begin again at a heap of stones and measured east 1/2 degree southerly 40 rods to a heap of stones and from thence north 30 degrees easterly 3 rods to the edge of the bank and so on the same course into the creek then from the first mentioned heap of stones west 17 degrees northerly through the lott unto the head. All the land between these lines and the last land divided unto William Soul and the land of said Allen to belong to them the said Nathaniel Soul, Jacob and Miles Soul.

Sixthly, we parted and set out to Nathan Soul that part whereon he now dwells to begin at said ancient bounds and to extend South 17 degrees easterly 103 rods and 1/3 lacking a foot to a heap of stones for the width of his said part and from them east 17 degrees southerly to the water and then west 17 degrees northerly from the bank 276 rods into the edge of the flag Swamp and from thence north 17 degrees easterly 26 rods & 1/2 and one foot and from thence west 17 degrees northerly unto the aforesaid lines, these lines to be the northerly extent of said Nathan's part.

Seventhly we parted and set out for Joseph Devol a piece joyning to said Nathan Souls and on the northerly side being in width 16 rods &1/2 and 1 foot extending *west 17 degrees northerly from the water up into the edge of the flug Swamp and is in length 376 rods.*

*Eighthly, we have parted and set out and divided unto William Soul a parcel of land at the north-easterly corner and is 39 rods wide and on the southern side is from a heap of stones from the bank west 10 degrees southerly round into the great swamp and from thence north 10 degrees westerly home to the northerly side and all the rest and remainder of said land on the west side of Coaxet River to belong to the said Nathaniel Soul, Jacob Soul and Miles Soul with the Island Cocherisnoset with which divisions we do by these presents own and acknowledge each of ourselves to have received our full parts and proportion of the share of divided lands first mentioned hereby binding ourselves and our heires and succesors to abide and stand by the partition and division as is hereby on the other side unto each of us divided and set out. In witness whereof we hereunto set our hands and seals this fourteenth day of May in the 7th year of her Majesties Reign, Anno Domini 1708.*

*Signed, sealed and delivered in the presence of Jonathan Devol, Robert Gifford, Thomas Taber, j Signed by Nathaniel Soul, Silvanus Soul, Jacob Soul, William Soul, Nathan Soul, Joseph Devol.*

*November 4th, 1709, Nathaniel Soul, Silvanus Soul, Jacob Soul, William Soul, Nathan Soul and Joseph Devol all personally appeared before me and acknowledged the above written instrument to be their act and deed.*

> – Seth Pope, Justice of the Peace.
> Entered July 3rd, 1711 by John Cary Recorder

## Appendix B – Dartmouth Properties Acquired and Sold by the Eddy Family in the Eighteenth Century

In 1747, Ichabod Eddy, recorded as being of Swansea at the time of this deed, bought a tract of land and salt meadow consisting of 114¾ acres from Timothy Soule for £1,500.[64] It was bounded northerly by Jacob Soule's land; westerly on Macomber's land; southerly partly on John (Timothy's brother) Soule's land and partly on the widow (Mary Gifford Soule, Timothy's mother) Soule's land; and easterly on the river.

In 1749, Ichabod Eddy of Dartmouth bought a second tract of land, containing 41 acres and 120 rods, from Stephen Soule. It was part of the land that was willed to Stephen by his father, Jacob Soule, who died in 1747/8. It was bounded easterly by land that Jacob Soule gave to Stephen's three brothers, Joseph, Nathaniel, and Benjamin; southerly by Ichabod Eddy's land; westerly by the remainder of Stephen Soule's land; and northerly by John Allen's land. Thus, this tract bordered, on its southern boundary, the land that Ichabod Eddy had purchased two years earlier from Timothy Soule, but it was well inland, separated from the river by the tracts of Joseph, Nathaniel, and Benjamin Soule.

In 1757, Ichabod Eddy of Dartmouth bought a third tract of land, this one containing 19 acres, from Wesson Soule for £20.[65] This tract was bounded on the north by Ichabod Eddy's own land; on the east by John Soule's land; on the south, partly by Nathaniel Soule's homestead and partly by John Soule's land; and westerly by land belonging to Robert Crossman. Thus, this was probably an addition on the south side of the original purchase in 1747 from Timothy Soule. It too was inland being at the west end of John Soule's land.

These three tracts totaled about 175 acres, with Ebenezer Eddy's homestead property and residence probably in the original tract. It was from these three tracts that the 100-acre parcel purchased by Paul Cuffe in 1799 and resold to Michael Wainer[66] in 1800 was carved out.[67]

In 1776, Phillip Allen sold two 20-acre parcels to Ichabod Eddy[68] and to his son, Henry Eddy.[69] The price for each was £100. They were parallel lots fronting easterly on the river. Ichabod's was the southern parcel, and it was bounded on the south by Benjamin Soule's land and on the north by Henry Eddy's land; both lots were bounded on the west and north by Phillip Allen's land. The sequence by which this property came into the ownership of Phillip Allen is described below. In 1799, Ebenezer Eddy, sold this 40-acre property, which he had inherited from his father, Ichabod Eddy, to Paul Cuffe.[70]

## Appendix C – Tracing the Origins of the "Allen Lot"

These notes seek to provide the background of the so-called "Allen lot" that was purchased by Paul Cuffe from Ebenezer Eddy in 1799.

Ralph Allen (1615-1691) came from Sandwich to Dartmouth in about 1663 and purchased large tracts of land, around what was later called Allens Pond, from Governor Bradford's widow, Alice; from Constant Southworth; and from Sarah Warren.[71] He distributed these tracts among his several sons: Benjamin, Increase, John, Zachariah, Joseph, and Ebenezer. Their holdings in the early eighteenth century can be seen on the maps derived from the field notes of Benjamin Crane, Benjamin Hammond, and Samuel Smith (henceforth known as Crane records).

The line of descent from Ralph Allen to Philip Allen, who sold the property to the Eddys in 1776, ran through his son, Joseph, (1642-1704) and Joseph's sons, Joseph (1667-1735) and John (1669-1754). These latter two Allens, Joseph and John, are frequently listed as J & J Allen in the Crane records. They owned a large 800-acre tract on the west side of the Acoaxet or east branch of the Westport River running from Main Road to the river, lying between two large tracts belong to Jacob Soule on the south and Joseph Peckham on the north, and opposite Cadman's Neck.

Joseph Allen (1667-1735) apparently was never married and had no children, so that his joint holdings seem to have passed to his younger brother, John. John Allen (1669-1754) married a cousin, Deborah Allen, and they had three children, only one of whom, Philip Allen (1717-1778), was a male.

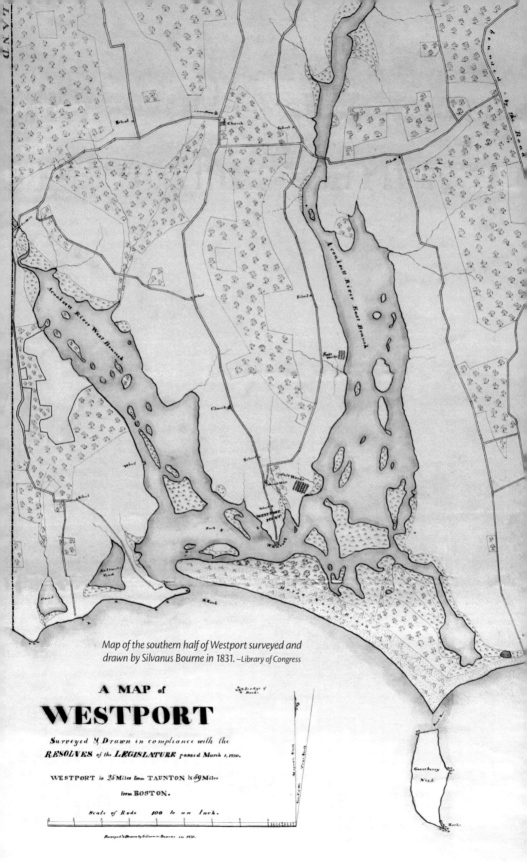

Map of the southern half of Westport surveyed and drawn by Silvanus Bourne in 1831. –Library of Congress

A MAP of
# WESTPORT
Surveyed & Drawn in compliance with the
RESOLVES of the LEGISLATURE passed March 1, 1830.

WESTPORT is 25 Miles from TAUNTON & 59 Miles from BOSTON.

Scale of Rods 100 to an Inch.

Surveyed & Drawn by Silvanus Bourne in 1831.

By his will dated 9 November, 1751,[72] John Allen appointed his son, Philip, as executor, and after granting some household items to his two daughters, Hannah Russell and Deborah Cornell, granted all the remainder part of his estate both real and personal in the township of Dartmouth to his son, Philip.

These properties probably included the tract mentioned above on the western shore of the Acoaxet River. This is the line by which Philip came to have a sizable holding of land in this area from which he sold two 20-acre adjacent tracts to Ichabod Eddy and Henry Eddy in 1776, two years before his death.[73] These two tracts were at the southeast corner of Philip Allen's holdings at that time as his property is cited as bounding the two Eddy tracts on the west and north, with the river on the east and Benjamin Soule's property on the south.

After Ichabod Eddy's death in 1795, his widow granted all rights of dower to her two sons, Zephaniah and Ebenezer Eddy.[74] There is a series of deeds in that same year that transferred the rights of several Eddy family members to Ebenezer Eddy as follows:

- *Zephaniah Eddy to Ebenezer Eddy for $290, land left to Zephaniah by his father, Ichabod, namely, "All my lands which I bought of Philip Allen lying east of Drift Way together with all lands I bought of my son Henry, lying eastward of Drift Way both of which lieth together bounded east by the river and west by Drift Way."[75]*

- *Henry and Ruth Eddy of Eastown, New York, to Ebenezer Eddy for $1,000, 20 acres bounded north by Daniel Tripp's land, East the River, South John Davis land and west by Drift Way, adjoining Ebenezer Eddy's land, with buildings, wharfs, etc.*

- *Nathan Eddy of Eastown, New York, to Ebenezer Eddy for $650, 60 acres, willed to him by his father, Ichabod Eddy, bounded north by Wesson Kirby's land, East by Isaac Soule heirs and Samuel Soule, South by Zephaniah Eddy and west by Benjamin Soule, Jacob Soule and Oliver Soule.*

The first of these appears to refer to the 40-acre "Allen Lot." The second and third appear to refer to two parts—20 plus 60 acres—of the 100-acre property that Ebenezer Eddy sold to Paul Cuffe in 1799, which Paul, in turn, sold to his brother-in-law, Michael Wainer, in 1800. The missing 20 acres of this 100-acre tract may be the tract referred to in the second item above as "adjoining Ebenezer Eddy's land," indicating that Ebenezer had already acquired it in his father's will.

# Notes

1. The story of this project in the district of Abyei in Sudan is told in the book by David Cole and Richard Huntington, *Between a Swamp and a Hard Place: Developmental Challenges in Remote Rural Africa.* Cambridge, Harvard University Press, 1997.

2. Fyfe, Christopher. *A History of Sierra Leone.* Oxford, Oxford Univ. Press, 1962. p. 105.

3. Wilson, Ellen Gibson. *Loyal Blacks.* New York, Capricorn Brooks, 1976. Wilson, Ellen Gibson. *John Clarkson and the African Adventure.* London, MacMillan Press, 1980; Thomas, Lamont D. *Rise to Be a People: A Biography of Paul Cuffe.* Urbana and Chicago, Univ. of Ill. Press, 1986; Braidwood, Stephen J. *Black Poor and White Philanthropists: London' Blacks and the Foundation of the Sierra Leone Settlement 1786-1791.* Liverpool University Press, 1994; Clifford, Mary Louise. *From*

*The Cuffes and Wainers established themselves along the western shore of the East Branch of the Westport River from just below Cadmen's Neck to halfway to Westport Point.*

*– from 1871 Map of Westport, Library of Congress*

96

*Slavery to Freetown: Black Loyalists after the American Revolution.* Jefferson, North Carolina, McFarland & Co. 1999; Campbell, James. *Middle Passages: African American Journeys to Africa, 1787-2005.* New York, The Penguin Press, 2006; Schama, Simon. *Rough Crossings: The Slaves, the British, and the American Revolution.* New York, HarperCollins, 2006. (Paperback); Pybus, Cassandra. *Epic Journeys of Freedom: Runaway Slaves of the American Rovolution and Their Global Quest for Liberty.* Boston, Beacon Press, 2006; Sidbury, James. *Becoming African in America: Race and Nation in the Early Black Atlantic.* Oxford, Oxford University Press, 2007.

4. The discussion in this section draws heavily on Braidwood and on Pybus, Chps. 5 and 7.

5. Peterson, John. *Province of Freedom: A History of Sierra Leone 1787-1870.* London, Faber and Faber, 1969. p.17. Clifford, *From Slavery to Freetown,* p.70 claims that "an eminent English Quaker doctor and abolitionist, Dr. John Fothergilll, sent Smeathman to Sierra Leone in 1771 to examine the possibility of establishing plantations there using black labor from England."

6. Fyfe, *History,* p. 15.

7. Ibid.

8. Ibid. p. 16.

9. Peterson, *Province of Freedom,* p.23.

10. Fyfe, p.19.

11. Peterson, p.27.

12. This section draws heavily on Pybus, Chps. 9 and 11.

13. Ibid. p. 80.

14. Ibid. p. 127

15. Ibid. Chp. 9.

16. The most extensive

discussion of the Maroons and their role in Sierra Leone that I have found is in C. Fyfe, *History,* Chps. III and IV. See also Schama, *Rough Crossings,* pp. 390-97, where he describes the Maroon history as "a strange, sad epic." Mavis Campbell, *The Maroons of Jamaica,1655-1796,* provides an interesting history of these ex-slaves before they came to Sierra Leone.

17. Fyfe, *History,* p.114.

18. Peterson, p.21.

19. Peterson, p.27.

20. Pybus, p. 149.

21. Pybus, p. 153 ff.

22. Ibid.

23. This process of deterioration is aptly described in Pybus' Chp. 11, entitled, "Promises Unfulfilled in Sierra Leone," and Wilson, *The Loyal Blacks.* Chp. 15, entitled "The Pursuit of Promises" and Chp. 19, entitled, "The Law of the Settlers."

24. Peterson, p. 63.

25. Ibid. p. 80.

26. This section relies heavily on Thomas, Chps. 7-9, and Sidbury, pp. 145, ff.

27. Sidbury, p. 151.

28. Thomas, p. 55. Macaulay, an ex-Governor of Sierra Leone, much disliked by the Nova Scotians, had returned to London and taken up the position of honorary secretary of the African Institute.

29. Sidbury, p. 154.

30. Ibid. p. 155.

31. Ibid.

32. Ibid. Also see the log of Paul Cuffe's trip to Washington to meet President Monroe in Wiggins, *Captain Paul Cuffe's Logs and Letters,* pp. 208-218.

33. Ibid. p. 160.

34. Ibid. pp. 163-4.

35. Paul Cuffe Papers, item 815.

36. Ibid. Items 81-103.

37. Ruth Cuffe's statement is presented and analyzed in Chapter Six.

38. A copy of the bill of sale is available on the <paulcuffe.org> website in the Documents section.

39. Alice Forbes Howland's, *Three Island: Pasque, Nashawena, Penikese,* 1964, has the following statement: "in 1751 Holder (Slocum) also acquired all the land on Nashawena, Cuttyhunk and Penikese," p. 60.

40. Intentions of Marriage. Paul Cuffe Manuscript Collection (PCMC), New Bedford Free Public Library (NBFPL), Book 1, Frames 79-102.

41. Records of Town of Dartmouth, Marriages, 1667-1787 and Deaths, 1687-1781, p. 48.

42. Pierce and Segel, Vol. II, p.197.

43. None of the children other than David appear in the vital records of either Dartmouth or Chilmark, so there is no specific record as to where they were born, but other records of the family seem to indicate that they were living on Cuttyhunk from sometime in 1750-51 until they moved to Dartmouth in 1767.

44. See Salvador, George. *The Black Yankee.* (1969), p. 12. And Thomas, Lamont. *Rise to Be a People.* (1986), p.5.

45. See Howland, Ibid., and Cronon, William. *Changes in the Land: Indians, Colonists, and the Ecology of New England.* New York: Farrar, Straus & Giroux, 1983.

46. See the inventory of the estate of Rebecca Slocum, Probate records for Bristol County, Taunton, MA. Items 1054-1094

47. Deed recorded in Town of Glocester, RI. Registry of Deeds Book 7, p. 252,

April 7, 1762. The deed was originally drawn up in Dartmouth, MA before Benjamin Akin, Justice of the Peace. The Lapham family was among the early settlers in Dartmouth and were staunch Quakers. Nicholas Lapham was probably a friend of Holder and John Slocum—both involved in helping Cuff Slocum gain his freedom.

48. Information on property transactions in Glocester,

RI was obtained from the Glocester town historian.

49. During the colonial period, British authorities adopted a "mercantilist" trade policy designed to restrict the outflow of their coinage. This policy was applied also to the North American colonies which resulted in a shortage of English money in the colonies. As a substitute the colonies made use of the Spanish milled silver

dollar that was minted in Mexico and other Spanish colonies in South America. Colonial authorities sought to maintain a stable exchange rate between the English pound and the Spanish dollar but this proved difficult and the exchange rates fluctuated over time and differed in the several colonies. See Jordan, Louis, "Colonial Currency" website.

50. PCMC, Scrap Book, p. 10.

*Detail of Buzzards Bay on this 1776 Map of New England shows Nashawena Island identified as "Slokums Island." The Slocum homestead was located near "Slokums Harbor" at the mouth of the Paskamansett River.*

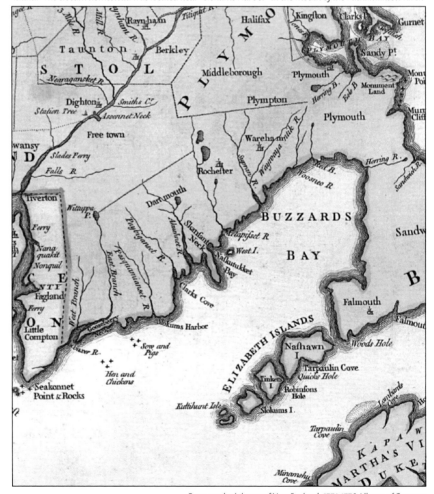

51. Enos Gifford purchased this and other adjoining properties from his father Christopher Gifford for £1,000 in 1736 (New Bedford Registry of Deeds [NBRD]) Book 4, p. 136. He sold this 120-acre property to Solomon Southwick of Newport, RI for 500 Spanish milled dollars on April 3, 1763 (NBRD, Book 7, p. 251); and Solomon Southwick sold the same property to David Brownell for 326 Spanish milled dollars on February 5, 1765 (NBRD, Book 8, p. 142.

52. The agreement to supply shingles to re-shingle the house is recorded in the PCMC Book 1, p. 8.

53. 1759, Enos Gifford to Rachel Wilbour, Bristol County Registry of Deeds (BCRD), Book 47, p. 240. Enos Gifford to Dorcas Manchester, (BCRD, Book 5, p. 537.)

54. It is probable that this Jonathan Soule, born in Dartmouth, December 10, 1710, and died there October 17, 1779, was a grandson of an original Mayflower settler, George Soule, who had also been one of the original proprietors who acquired large tracts of land along the South Coast from the Wampanoags in 1652. Source: Sprague, Waldo Chamberlain, "The Dartmouth Branch of the Soule Family," in *The American Genealogist*, Volume, 39, #12 (January 1963).

55. Gradoia, Eric, "Remarks on the Cuffe Slocum house, 761 Old County Road, Westport, Massachusetts." Report prepared for the Westport Historical Society in 2016.

56. See also Wertz, Richard, *The Head of Westport:*

*A Brief History and a Walking Tour Guide to Its Historic Houses.* Westport Historical Commission, rev. ed. from 2009, p. 34.

57. A plan for crop planting was drawn up by John Slocum in 1780 showing a pattern for planting seeds four feet apart in mounds, 160 mounds per acre. This may have been for corn fields. See PCMC, item 18.

58. In modern times there is a very popular fruit farm, Dartmouth Orchards, located one mile to the east on Old County Road.

59. Pierce, Andrew, and Segel, Jerome. *Wampanoag Families of Martha's Vineyard*, Heritage Books, 2016, p.197.

60. Bristol County Probate Records, Vol. 22-23, 1771-1775, Item 125-126, pp. 225-227.

61. The most easily accessible site is the Town of Westport, Massachusetts website: Historical Documents: Paul Cuffe Personal and Family Papers: Items 81 to 103.

62. This chapter presents a modified version of a paper entitled: "New Revelations from Old Deeds: The Property Holdings of Cuff Slocum, Paul Cuffe and Michael Wainer" by David C. Cole, Richard Gifford and Betty F. Slade, with maps by Raymond C. Shaw, presented at the symposium, *Paul Cuffe (1759-1817) Following His Footsteps*, Westport, September 16, 2017.

63. Spelling of the name Sowle is sometimes Soule or Soul. In this text we have used whichever spelling was used in the underlying document or map.

64. NBRD, 1747, Book 5, p. 474. Timothy Soule (1714-1772)

was a son of Nathan (1680-1736), a grandson of George (1639-1704) and a brother of John (1707-1771).

65. NBRD, 1757, Book 7, pp. 66-67. Wesson Soule (1735-1825) was a son of Nathaniel (1681-1766), and grandson of Nathaniel (1637-1699 or 1702?).

66. NBRD, 1800, Book 16, p. 390.

67. NBRD, 1799, Book 15, p. 169.

68. NBRD, 1776, Book 10, pp. 16-17.

69. NBRD, 1776, Book 10, p. 17

70. NBRD, 1799, Book 15, p. 170.

71. According to Beverly Morrison Glennon, *Dartmouth, The Early History of a Massachusetts Coastal Town*, p. 110, these properties were later divided among his descendants. The former Warren property, Barney's Joy, was left to Ralph's son Ebenezer. The former Bradford property was divided between his sons Zachariah and Increase. One-third part of the former Southworth land was granted to his son, Joseph, by a deed dated January 18, 1678-79. One-third part of the former Southworth land was granted to Joseph's sons, Joseph Jr. and John Allen at the same time.

72. His will was admitted to probate on July 2, 1754.

73. The two deeds for these transactions are in Book 10, pp. 16-17, February 22, 1777.

74. NBRD, March 30, 1795, Book 14, p. 531.

75. NBRD, March 30, 1795, Book 14, p. 531.

# Index

# Bibliography

## Publications

Bosworth, Janet. *Cuttyhunk and the Elizabeth Islands from 1602*. Cuttyhunk Historical Society, Cuttyhunk, Massachusetts. 1993.

Bolster, W. Jeffrey. *Black Jacks: African American Seamen in the Age of Sail*.

Braidwood, Stephen J. *Black Poor and White Philanthropists: London' Blacks and the Foundation of the Sierra Leone Settlement 1786-1791*. Liverpool University Press, 1994.

Bullard, John M. *The Rotches*. New Bedford, 1947. Cambridge, Harvard Univ. Press, 1997.

Campbell, James. *Middle Passages: African American Journeys to Africa, 1787-2005*. New York, The Penguin Press, 2006.

Campbell, Mavis C.. *The Maroons of Jamaica 1655-1796, A History of Resistence, Collaboration & Betrayal*. Granby, Mass. Berfin & Garvey Publishers, 1988.

Campbell, Mavis C.. *Back to Africa: George Ross & the Maroons, From Nova Scotia to Sierra Leone*. Trenton, Africa World Press, 1993.

Clifford, Mary Louise. *From Slavery to Freetown: Black Loyalists after the American Revolution*. Jefferson, NC, McFarland & Co. 1999.

Cole, David C. and Richard Huntington. *Between a Swamp and a Hard Place: Developmental Challenges in Remote Rural Africa*. Cambridge, Harvard Institute for International Development, 1997.

Cuffe, Paul. Paul Cuffe Manuscript Collection at the New Bedford Free Public Library. New Bedford, Massachusetts.

Devlin, Edward W. *A Man Born on Purpose: Captain Paul Cuffe of Westport, Mariner, Educator, African-American, 1759-1817*. Westport Historical Society, 1997.

Diamond, Arthur, *Paul Cuffe: Merchant and Abolitionist*. New York, Chelsea House Publishers, 1989.

Equiano, Olaudah. *The Interesting Narrative and Other Writings*. Edited by Vincent Carretta. London, Penguin, 2003.

Fyfe, Christopher. *A History of Sierra Leone*. Oxford, Oxford Univ. Press, 1962.

Glennon, Beverley Morrison, *Dartmouth: The Early History of a Massachusetts Coastal Town*. New Bedford, American Printing

Grover, Kathryn. *The Fugitive's Gibraltar: Escaping Slaves and Abolitionism in New Bedford, Massachusetts*. Amherst, Univ. of Mass. Press, 2001.

Howland, Alice Forbes. *Three Islands: Pasque, Nashawena and Penikese*. Boston, Pinkham Press, 1964.

Jordan, Winthrop D. *White over Black: American Attitudes Toward the Negro, 1550-1812*. Chapel Hill, Univ. of North Carolina Press, 1968.

Peterson, John. *Province of Freedom: A History of Sierra Leone 1787-1870*. London, Faber and Faber, 1969.

Pierce, Andrew & Jerome D. Segel. *Wampanoag Families of Martha's Vineyard*. Heritage Books, 2016.

Pybus, Cassandra. *Epic Journeys of Freedom: Runaway Slaves of the American Revolution and Their Global Quest for Liberty*. Boston, Beacon Press, 2006.

Rawley, James A. with Stephen D. Behrendt. *The Transatlantic Slave Trade: A History, revised edition*. Lincoln, Univ. of Nebraska Press, 2005.

Rappleye, Charles. *Sons of Providence: The Brown Brothers, the Slave Trade, and the American Revolution*. New York, Simon & Schuster, 2006.

Salvador, George. *Paul Cuffe, The Black Yankee, 1759-1817*. New Bedford, Reynolds-DeWalt Printing, Inc. 1969.

Schama, Simon. *Rough Crossings: The Slaves, the British, and the American Revolution*. New York, HarperCollins, 2006.

Sherwood, H. N. "Paul Cuffe." *Journal of Negro History* (1923): 153-229.

Sidbury, James. *Becoming African in America: Race and Nation in the Early Black Atlantic*. Oxford, Oxford University Press, 2007.

Slocum, Charles Elihu. *A Short History of the Slocums, Slocumbs and Slocombs of America, Genealogical and Biographical, from 1637 to 1881*. Syracuse, NY, author-published, 1882.

Sprague, Waldo Chamberlain, "The Dartmouth Branch of the Soule Family," in *The American Genealogist, Volume, 39, #12* (Jan. 1963).

Thomas, Lamont D. *Paul Cuffe: Black Entrepreneur and Pan-Africanist*. Urbana and Chicago, Univ of Ill. Press, 1988. (Paperback version of previous citation.)

Thomas, Lamont D. *Rise to Be a People: A Biography of Paul Cuffe*. Urbana and Chicago, Univ. of Ill. Press, 1986.

Wertz, Richard, *The Head of Westport: A Brief History and a Walking Tour Guide to Its Historic Houses*. Westport Historical Commission, Revised edition, 2009.

Westgate, Michael, *Captain Paul Cuffe (1759-1817) A One-Man Civil Rights Movement*, Museum of the National Center of Afro-American Artists and Education and Resources Group, Boston, 1989. Unpublished mimeographed papers.

Wiggins, Rosalind Cobb. *Captain Paul Cuffe's Logs and Letters, 1808-1817: A Black Quaker's "Voice from within the Veil"*. Washington, Howard Univ. Press. 1996

Wilson, Ellen Gibson. *The Loyal Blacks*. New York, Capricorn Books. 1976.

Wilson, Ellen Gibson. *John Clarkson and the African Adventure*. London, MacMillan Press, 1980.

Winch, Julie. *A Gentleman of Color: The Life of James Forten*. Oxford, Oxford University Press, 2002.

Worth, Henry. Papers, Box 16, Sg-1, Series F, SS 3, Vol 1, P. 121. New Bedford Whaling Museum Library.

Vital Records of the Town of Dartmouth.

## Documentary Sources:

Bristol County Registry of Deeds, Taunton Office and New Bedford Office.

Bristol County Probate Records, Taunton, MA

Proprietors Land Records, Dartmouth, Vols. 1 & 2, digital copies of original documents held by the New Bedford Registry of Deeds

New Bedford Free Public Library, New Bedford, MA

New Bedford Whaling Museum Library, New Bedford, MA

The Field Notes of Benjamin Crane, Benjamin Hammond and Samuel Smith, Reproduced in Facsimile from the Original Notes of Survey of Lands of the Proprietors of Dartmouth. 1910, New Bedford, Mass. New Bedford Free Public Library. The Benjamin Crane Maps are based on the Field Notes and were created by Henry Worth.

Westport Historical Commission website, Paul Cuffe page.

Westport Monthly Meeting, Men's Minutes, 3-17-1797 to 3-17-1836, and Acoaxett Monthly Meeting, Births, Deaths and Marriages, 1766-1882, from the Special Collections Section of the W. E. B. Du Bois Library, University of Massachusetts, Amherst, MA.

# About the Authors

David Cole grew up in Michigan, attended Deep Springs College, spent a year in China (1946-47) training young Chinese men to use and repair tractors, graduated from Cornell University in 1950 with a degree in Far Eastern Studies, served in Korea in 1951-52 and earned a Ph.D. in economics at the University of Michigan in 1959. In his professional career, he specialized on economic development in Asia and was affiliated with the Harvard Economics Faculty for nearly three decades. He co-authored ten books starting with Korean Economic Development: The Interplay of Politics and Economics, with Princeton Lyman, published by Harvard University Press in 1970, and ending with *Building a Modern Financial System: The Indonesian Experience*, co-authored with Betty Slade and published by Cambridge University Press in 1996. His latest book, *Lucky Me: Engaging a World of Challenges and Opportunities*, self-published in 2014, retraces both his personal and professional experiences over eight decades. Since settling in Westport, he has focused on environmental preservation and historical research.

Richard Gifford is a native and current resident of Little Compton, RI. He has conducted genealogical research for several decades, in recent years focusing on the Cuffe/Wainer family and other historic families of color of the South Coast area. His legal background has facilitated his researching title histories of the Cuffe and Wainer properties. Over the past decade he has given numerous presentations to local organizations on topics relating to history and genealogy. He holds an A.B. degree in history from Brown University and a J.D. degree from the University of Connecticut School of Law.

Betty Slade, of southern heritage, early on became a civil rights advocate for people of color, culminating in work with the New Bedford Historical Society for the last ten years to celebrate the lives of Paul Cuffe and Michael Wainer. She attended Georgetown School of Foreign Service and earned her Ph.D. in Economics at Vanderbilt. She taught at several universities and worked as an economist in Turkey, other parts of the Middle East, England, Indonesia, and several countries in Africa and South America. Eventually retiring in Westport, she became active in historic preservation, especially of historic burial grounds, and has conducted many interviews to record local history. She has remained actively involved with the Westport Historical Society and the Westport Community Preservation Committee for many years.

Raymond Shaw, a Westport resident, Massachusetts native and graduate of Massachusetts College of Art, served as a military officer in the Vietnam War and worked for forty years with multinational corporations in the marketing and design professions. In recent years, he has offered his creative talents to Westport historical initiatives.